You,_____,
like Suzan Ziglar Witmeyer, can spend eternity in Heaven if you will confess with your mouth that Jesus is Lord and believe in your heart that God raised Him from death (Romans 10:9), not because of what you did or did not do, but because of what He did on the cross.

CONFESSIONS OF A
GRIEVING
CHRISTIAN

CONFESSIONS OF A

GRIEVING
CHRISTIAN

ZIG ZIGLAR

THOMAS NELSON PUBLISHERS
Nashville

Published in Nashville, Tennessee, by Thomas Nelson, Inc.

Scripture quotations noted NKJV are from THE NEW KING JAMES VERSION. Copyright © 1979, 1980, 1982, Thomas Nelson, Inc., Publishers.

Scripture quotations noted KJV are from THE KING JAMES VERSION of the Bible.

Scripture quotations noted TLB are from THE LIVING BIBLE, copyright 1971 by Tyndale House Publishers, Wheaton, IL. Used by permission.

Scripture quotations noted NASB are from the NEW AMERICAN STANDARD BIBLE ®, © Copyright The Lockman Foundation 1960, 1962, 1963, 1968, 1971, 1972, 1973, 1975, 1977. Used by permission.

Scripture quotations noted NIV are from the HOLY BIBLE: NEW INTERNATIONAL VERSION ®. Copyright © 1973, 1978, 1984 by International Bible Society. Used by permission of Zondervan Publishing House. All rights reserved.

Scripture quotations noted NLT are from the *Holy Bible*, New Living Translation, copyright © 1996. Used by permission of Tyndale House Publishers, Inc., Wheaton, Illinois 60189. All rights reserved.

Library of Congress Cataloging-in-Publication Data
Ziglar, Zig.
    Confessions of a grieving Christian / Zig Ziglar.
        p.   cm.
    ISBN 0-8407-9182-8
    1. Grief—Religious aspects—Christianity. 2. Children—Death—Religious aspects—Christianity. 3. Ziglar, Zig. 4. Witmeyer, Suzan Ziglar, 1949–1995. 5. Consolation. I. Title.
BV4907.Z54   1998
248.8'66—dc21   98-29517
                                                                              CIP

Printed in the United States of America
1 2 3 4 5 6 BVG 03 02 01 00 99 98

Dedicated to the memory of
SUZAN ZIGLAR WITMEYER
Beautiful, much-loved daughter,
loving wife,
devoted mother, and
faithful servant of the Lord Jesus Christ

Contents

Foreword   ix

Acknowledgments   xi

Introduction: Meet My Daughter Suzan   xv

1   "She's Gone . . ."   1

2   The Loss of Suzan—Our Beloved
Firstborn Daughter   9

3   A Wave of Emotions   29

4   Facing the Fears of Death   41

5   The Difference Christ Makes   53

6   Facing the *Why* Questions   63

7   No Doubt About It!   77

8   Heaven's Glory   87

9   Appreciating All of God's Miracle Moments   105

10   Comfort and Joy from Prayer and the Word   119

11 We Grieve in Different Ways 133

12 Comforting the Grieving 141

13 Giving to Others Out of Your Grief 157

14 Keeping the Relationship Alive 173

15 God's Strength and Grace to Continue with
    Life and Work 183

16 The Loss and the Love 193

17 Why We Feel No Regret and No Guilt 201

18 Ongoing Aftershocks of Grief 215

19 Choosing the Best Memories 229

20 Can a Person Prepare in Advance for Grief? 241

    Postlude 247

    Appendix: Suzan Ziglar Witmeyer Funeral Service 249

    About the Author 265

FOREWORD

ZIG ZIGLAR IS known around the world as a great communicator. His name is synonymous with success. Multiplied thousands have been encouraged, educated, and motivated by his inspirational words. But Zig's dynamic communication is far more than words.

As his pastor, I have had the privilege to know this man well. He and his lovely wife, Jean, are active members of our church. So when the Ziglars walked through the valley of the shadow with their precious daughter Suzan, it was my privilege to be by their side.

Zig is the most "up" person I know, but then he was "down." The man who took us to the top and beyond was looking at the bottom. It was then, facing one of life's dark times, that Zig's faith shone brightly. You see, through the years, this godly man has been telling us that true happiness is found in Jesus Christ. He has taught us to look beyond our problems and see possibilities. To see, through pain, the promises of God.

So I was not surprised that Zig and Jean faced the raw reality of death and grief with faith, hope, and love. Though the sorrow was deep and agonizing, they stood firm upon God's Word and the deep convictions developed over years and years of trusting and obeying God.

When you read *Confessions of a Grieving Christian,* you will realize, more than ever, that Zig's faith is real and that his fire still burns. This book is not about sentimentality. It deals with one of the most difficult subjects known to mankind. The message is honest, thoughtful, and spiritual.

Zig allows us to look into his soul, and he shares his grief that we might discover God's grace. It was a painful experience for him to write this book, but this triumphant believer wanted others to be comforted and helped by his loss. I predict that this will become Zig's most loved book. Grief touches us all. The message shared in these pages will embrace you, comfort you, and strengthen you. You will learn some of life's most important lessons from a man who has lived what he writes.

Thank you, Zig, for opening up your grieving heart and pouring out your personal testimony of God's love and power. You have given us something that will last forever.

Dr. Jack Graham
Senior Pastor
Prestonwood Baptist Church
Dallas, Texas

ACKNOWLEDGMENTS

I T'S ALWAYS DIFFICULT to properly address all of the individuals involved in the creation of any work and thank them for the contributions they have made. So many have been so significant that words seem inadequate. I know we've had the countless prayers of people I will never meet and many others whom I know only casually. There is no question but that God heard their prayers as this project extended over a three-year period.

I begin with my editor, who is my youngest daughter, Julie Ziglar Norman. Without her insight and her love for her sister and for me, many elements of this book would have been less meaningful. Both of us have shed many tears in the process of the writing. Interestingly enough, Julie's tears came less during the assembling of the book for which she was primarily responsible and more after the technical aspects were completed when she read through the book as a whole rather than as a project. She cried throughout the final reading. What a marvelous help she has been, and what a delight she is to work with!

I'm deeply indebted to my faithful executive assistant of twenty-plus years, Laurie Magers, who is as close to being a member of the family as one can get without being a family member. She loved Suzan deeply, and she wept as she transcribed my dictation. Her help and insight were invaluable.

I have much gratitude for the expertise of editor Jan Dargatz. She beautifully reworked the format of this book during a time of intense personal grieving over the sudden, tragic loss of her father. I believe that her sensitivity to the grieving experience greatly enhanced this work.

Editor Brian Hampton has now worked with me on three books, and I can't thank him enough for the many hours he devotes to seeing our books through from start to finish. I am always more than pleased with the end results!

My son-in-law Jim Norman, Julie's husband, who contributed the diary of events leading up to Suzan's death, was very helpful and added considerably to the book.

My pastor, Dr. Jack Graham, suggested the title for the book, contributed the Foreword, and allowed me to quote from some of his sermons. Dr. Paige Patterson, at a critical time in my life after Suzan's death, offered some extremely valuable counsel, as did Dr. Ike Reighard, Dr. James Merritt, Dr. O. S. Hawkins, Dr. W. A. Criswell, and Dr. John Maxwell. In the fifteen days before Suzan's death, no one could have been more loving, kind, considerate, or compassionate than John and Charlotte West, who are a big part of Prestonwood Baptist Church. They were magnificent in their visits, faithfulness in prayer, and encouragement. Jim Lewis, Suzan's pastor, a rock of faith, was encouraging and helpful to us, as was Michael FinCannon, who has been a friend and counselor to our family for many years. Others who have been helpful through their writing, speaking, and personal encouragement are Neal Jeffrey, Steve Brown, Dan Bellus, Ron Ezinga, Don Hawkins, Dr. Howard Hendricks, George Sparks, Wilson McKinney, Mike Ingram, Dan and Cay Bolin, Samuel Henning, Dina and Jack Landers, Larry and Lisa Carpenter, Mark and Margie Warren, Gam and Rebecca Greer, Thelma Wells, Rodney Gage, and David Hawkins.

The love and support of each of my children and my sons- and daughter-in-law have been factors in the creation and completion of this book, as have been the anonymous sources that I used—each contributed a part to this work. To all of you, I am indebted and deeply grateful for the contribution you made.

As always, the one who means the most to me is my beautiful wife, Jean, whose constant love, encouragement, support, and empathetic expressions of understanding throughout the process of writing this book have made this labor of love possible. Her subtle but significant changes in the thoughts and words added much to its spiritual depth.

INTRODUCTION

Meet My Daughter Suzan

In order that you might come to know and feel just who Suzan was and why we loved her so much, I want to introduce her to you through a story that she wrote a couple of years before her death and well before any of us realized that she was already feeling the impact of an illness that had not yet been diagnosed. I believe her heart, sensitivity, and passion, as well as her beautiful use of words, will help you in a more intimate way to know the Suzan we all loved. At the same time you will get a feel for who I am and why I felt compelled to write this book.

The New Jacket
By: Suzan Ziglar Witmeyer

It was a brisk, late fall afternoon in Mississippi. The year was 1936 and the Depression raged. Hilary Ziglar shifted his weight to his right foot and then back again as he counted his money. He stood on a street corner in downtown Yazoo City. It had been an unusually good week for him in the peanut business. He had sold 87 bags of peanuts at a profit of a penny a bag.

A gust of wind sent Hilary's hands diving for the pockets of his overalls as a shiver ran the length of his frail, nine-year-old body. Mississippi weather in late October got very uncomfortable for a boy dressed only in well-worn cotton. "Eighty-seven cents," he thought, "in one week. I'm going to do it, I'm going to Warren's now!" With that he stood a little straighter, squared his shoulders, tucked in his chin and began a little march-jog step down Main Street in the direction of Dement Warren's Haberdasher.

Hilary's father, Silas, had been a plantation overseer until his death, four years earlier, of a stroke following a serious bout with Malaria. The family had been in desperate straits ever since. That's why Hilary was downtown working while his school friends played sandlot ball. Young Hilary Hinton was as fully employed as a nine-year-old could be and still go to school. He sold peanuts on the streets of Yazoo City, for Uncle Joe's Peanuts, every day after school, and on Saturdays he worked in Mr. John Anderson's grocery store.

Inside Warren's, Hilary carefully counted out his 87 cents and pointed to the window where a tan, button-down jacket was displayed. "That's the one I want, Ma'am," he said to the sales clerk. Glancing quickly at the price tag the clerk said, "That's right, Hilary, 87 cents, right on the money!"

"Yes, Ma'am!" he said proudly.

The clerk removed the jacket from its hanger and carefully folded it. She then wrapped it in a large piece of brown paper and tied it with string. The wrapping completed, she handed the package to the shyly beaming boy who then headed for the door.

Outside again, Hilary set out for the Black and White Store to see his sister, Turah. As he entered the store he was greeted with a warm, "Hi there, Short Boy!" He grimaced slightly at his nickname but smiled as his brown eyes met the identical eyes of his lovely sister. "Hi, Sis," he said, "guess what I've got here?" "Well I don't rightly know, Boy, did you pick up somethin' for Mama?" she asked. "Nope, I did not pick up anything for Mama, I bought this for my ownself with my own money that I made THIS week!" "And you only nine years old, Short Boy. Let me see!" Turah begged. "Oh no you don't, Sis, nobody's gonna see this before Mama, and that's that!" Hilary said. "Well I just don't know what the world is coming to when a nine-year-old boy can go out and buy goodness-knows-what brand spankin' new!"

Glancing at the clock Hilary saw that it was almost supper time. "Gotta go, Sis," he said, "almost time to eat." With that he walked out into the brisk evening air, the precious package tucked firmly under his right arm. Turah watched sadly from the window as the slender form of her little brother faded into the night. "Take care, Short Boy," she whispered.

Traveling through the neat streets of Yazoo City, young Hilary started to jog. It wasn't that he was in a hurry, he simply was getting very cold. His thin cotton shirt was no match for the moist, cold, late October weather. He would not consider opening his package and wearing his new jacket. On and on he jogged, crossing the bayou and heading for the railroad tracks and home. The mile-and-a-half journey seemed endless. His ears began to tingle and his toes were going numb, but still he jogged, coatless, his paper bundle safe under his arm.

Lila Westcott Ziglar moved with great economy around her simple kitchen. Mother of eleven living children, widow, she had no steps to waste. Life was a grueling round of work and more work. She lived for Sundays, a time to worship her God and to rest. Today was Friday, one more day to go. Now, where was Hilary?

Oh, how she worried about her children, especially her younger ones. These last four years without Silas had been brutal. She remembered so clearly the move into town after his death and her sad farewell at the graves of her husband and baby, graves made only one week apart. She didn't pretend to know the mind of God, she accepted what was handed to her, trusting in Him completely. Oh, but she hated sending her little ones out to work!

"Now where is Hilary?" Lila muttered as she shoved another pan of biscuits into the oven. A layer of flour coated her long, slim fingers, while her left cheek sported a grainy, Florida-shaped configuration of the white powder.

Just then she heard the familiar thud of the front door and knew Hilary was home at last. "Boy," she called, "where have you been? You know how I worry." At the sound of heavy breathing she realized he had entered the room. She looked up and was startled by the intensity of his smile. "Why, Hilary," she said, "what have you done? Why are you smiling like that?" "Look, Mama," he said, "look what I bought with my own money." A package wrapped in brown paper and tied with string materialized in front of her.

Her fingers trembled slightly as she freed the jacket from its bonds. Little bits of flour floated towards the linoleum as the paper fell away and the jacket came into full view. "Why, Boy," she said with a tone of wonder, "you've gone and bought yourself a coat, a new coat, all by yourself. I don't know what to say, Hilary. I'm proud of you, Son."

The proud boy trying on his new jacket for the first time did not notice the unnatural brightness of his mother's eyes as she fought to hold back her tears.

Fifty years after my father bought his first jacket he told me this story. When he got to the part where he showed my grandmother the jacket, he was overcome with emotion. His respect for his mother was so great, his need to help his family in some concrete way was so enormous, that a half century could not dim the feelings. My heart ached as I saw the little, too-thin Delta boy with tears in his eyes. I was reminded once again that my father will always remain that little, fatherless boy from Yazoo City in some significant ways.

"SHE'S GONE . . ."

ON MAY 10, 1949, after thirty hours of labor, a nurse said to me, "It's a girl, Mr. Ziglar." Jean Suzanne Ziglar had arrived in this world of ours. We called her Suzan. My joy knew no bounds.

On May 12, 1995, a doctor said to us, "Medically speaking, there's nothing else we can do. She has only a matter of hours before she goes into eternity. We will do everything we can to make her comfortable."

On May 13, 1995, at 9:45 A.M., a nurse said, "She's gone." Those words broke my heart.

It is impossible to describe fully the grief that overwhelmed my family and me at the death of our beloved firstborn daughter. Nothing had prepared me for the intensity of pain and sorrow I experienced.

In the past, I had grieved deeply when my mother and some of my brothers and sisters died. I do not remember my father or his death, but I have grieved the fact that I did not know my father. I have grieved over the deaths of close friends, and I have also grieved as I have watched close friends grieve over the loss of their family members and friends.

Even so, there is no grief that I have experienced that has come close to my grief over the loss of our child.

Throughout our months and years of grieving, faith has been the redeeming force that has enabled us to bear the pain and continue to live in victory. As has often been said, when we don't know God's head, we can trust His heart. We know that not only is God too wise to make a mistake, but He is too loving to cause one of His own to endure needless pain. In short, the very process of grief is given to us by a loving heavenly Father. God uses grief to heal us, strengthen us in our faith, and cause us to grow in our relationship with Him. While I do not believe that God causes the circumstances that result in our grief, I do believe that God uses grief as a process to show His compassion toward us, to teach us, and to bring us into greater wholeness.

I certainly have seen that come to pass in my life in the last few years.

Out of my grief has come a faith that far exceeds anything that I had before Suzan went home to the Lord.

Out of my grief has come a deeper love for my beautiful wife. Prior to Suzan's death, I doubt if I thought a deeper love was possible since I already loved my wife so deeply, and yet a deeper love has developed.

Out of my grief has come a deeper love for my other children, again, a love that exceeds the great love I already felt for them.

Out of my grief has come a deeper love for other members of my family, including my sons-in-law, my daughter-in-law, my grandchildren, cousins, nieces, nephews, and other relatives.

Out of my grief has come a sense of urgency to be more

effective in my witness for Christ and to pray more diligently for guidance that I might be doing all that the Lord has for me to do in this life.

EACH OF US WILL GRIEVE—AT SOME TIME, OVER SOMEONE

If we live long enough, each one of us will have the opportunity to learn the lessons related to grief—if, indeed, we choose to learn them. No one is immune from the *fact* of grief. Grief is woven throughout the tapestry of life.

The word *loss* is perhaps the most potent word to describe the cause for grief. My 1828 Noah Webster dictionary says that *grief* "is the pain of mind, produced by loss, misfortune, injury, or evils of any kind; sorrow; regret." Grief comes to us all at some point in our lives, and it comes in varying degrees related to a wide variety of losses. If you consider all who are experiencing loss in our world today, you can begin to see the extent of grief. It is pervasive. Virtually everyone is experiencing some type of grief to some degree.

There is considerable grief in our world today over the loss of jobs. When a job is lost, relationships that are important are often lost, and grief results. Athletes grieve when their careers come to an end and they have to bid their teammates good-bye. Divorce frequently has a period of grief associated with it because the death of a marriage is just that, the death of a relationship. Parents frequently grieve when their children go to college or marry, move to another city, enlist in the armed services, or simply move out of the family home into a place of their own. When our son, Tom, our youngest child, went to college—even though it was only an hour's drive away and we knew we

3

would be seeing him regularly—we experienced grief that all of our children had "left the nest." The first night that Tom was away, I have to confess that I experienced an intense feeling of loneliness and sadness as I walked down the hallway past the door to his bedroom.

Many people grieve over the loss of a pet. I vividly recall my grief when a little Scottie that we had for only a brief period of time was run over. I remember the grief I felt when a cat of many years, which we named B. W. Person, had to be put to sleep. My daughters particularly have grieved when a family pet or a horse they have owned or ridden, or even one belonging to a close friend, had to be put down.

We feel grief at the misfortune of others, particularly our close friends. We grieve when loved ones experience the loss of a special treasure. We feel grief at tragic misfortunes.

We also grieve for our own misfortunes, follies, and vices, as well as those of our children. There are times when grief follows in the wake of a mistake or rebellious act, either ours or that of someone we love. The prophet and high priest Samuel took Saul's rebellion very personally. In 1 Samuel 15:10–11 (NKJV) we read, "Now the word of the LORD came to Samuel, saying, 'I greatly regret that I have set up Saul as king, for he has turned back from following Me, and has not performed My commandments.' And it grieved Samuel, and he cried out to the LORD all night."

The Scriptures tell us in Hebrews 13:17 (NKJV), "Obey those who rule over you, and be submissive, for they watch out for your souls, as those who must give account. Let them do so with joy and not with grief, for that would be unprofitable for you." Notice here that grief has been associated with the sin of others—rather than *cause* grief for others through our rebellion against God, we are advised by the writer of Hebrews to *give* others joy.

Noah Webster also noted that *grief* is "the pain of mind occasioned by our own misconduct; sorrow or regret that we have done wrong. We feel grief when we have offended or injured a friend, and the consciousness of having offended the Supreme Being fills the penitent heart with the most poignant grief."

Yes, grief is a natural response to the loss of our innocence or our obedience before God. When we disobey God, we always lose. First and foremost, we lose some of the intimacy and fellowship we have enjoyed with our Creator.

GOD GRIEVES WITH US

Are you aware that God Himself grieves? The psalmist asserted, "How often they provoked Him in the wilderness, and grieved Him in the desert" (Ps. 78:40 NKJV). God grieves when His people rebel or refuse to obey. In Ephesians 4:30–31 (NKJV) we are told, "Do not grieve the Holy Spirit of God, by whom you were sealed for the day of redemption. Let all bitterness, wrath, anger, clamor, and evil speaking be put away from you, with all malice."

I find comfort in reading that God the Father, God the Son, and God the Holy Spirit all grieve when we refuse to obey and rebel against Him. If our heavenly Father grieves at our losses as well as our misconduct, surely grief is not only natural but also desirable.

Grief is desirable? Yes—because, I believe, it brings us to the stark realization of two things:

First, grief brings us to the point of realizing the vastness of our love, and of God's love for us. Grief gives us a renewed awareness of our capacity both to give and to receive love.

The apostle Paul knew about grief: "Out of much affliction

and anguish of heart I wrote to you, with many tears, not that you should be grieved, but that you might know the love which I have so abundantly for you" (2 Cor. 2:4 NKJV). Grief is perhaps the most profound way of expressing love.

The intensity of grief is directly related to the intensity of love. The more we love a person we have lost, the greater our grief.

Second, grief puts us into a position to trust God alone for our healing and restoration. In cases of disobedience, grief compels us to repent and receive forgiveness.

God both knows and cares that we grieve. He awaits our turning to Him for comfort and healing. From Psalm 56:8, we learn that God collects our tears in a bottle—God takes note of our sadness and remembers it! And in the moment we turn to Him, God acts to begin the healing process in our hearts.

Not only is grief natural and godly, but Jeremiah declared,

> *O LORD, are not Your eyes on the truth?*
> *You have stricken them,*
> *But they have not grieved;*
> *You have consumed them,*
> *But they have refused to receive correction.*
> *They have made their faces harder than rock;*
> *They have refused to return. (Jer. 5:3 NKJV)*

Jeremiah's message to us is quite clear—when we are "stricken," we are wise to grieve any error that may be associated with our loss and then to receive help, even correction, from the Lord. Above all, we are to maintain a softness of heart and to turn to the Lord rather than become hardened and turn away from God. The healing and wholeness that we desire in the aftermath of a loss are to be found only if we turn to the Lord with a trusting, obedient, "soft" heart.

In Lamentations 3:31–33 (NIV), the prophet Jeremiah offered these additional words:

> *For men are not cast off by the Lord forever.*
> *Though he brings grief, he will show compassion,*
>   *so great is his unfailing love.*
> *For he does not willingly bring affliction*
>   *or grief to the children of men.*

The Lord is merciful to us in our grief. He always proves Himself worthy of the trust He calls us to have in Him.

A BENEFIT FROM GRIEF

No matter how deeply we hurt or how much pain we suffer in our grief, God has something good for us in the midst of it. He Himself is present, and He is good. The good lessons we learn that are for our eternal benefit, the vast and good love we experience from others and from God, and the good trust we develop are all positive outcomes of a grief that is given over to God.

To express this *goodness* that can come from grief is the very reason for this book.

I wrote *Confessions of a Happy Christian* primarily for my daughter Suzan in hopes that she would accept Jesus Christ as her personal Savior and commit her life to following Him as her Lord. I write *Confessions of a Grieving Christian* in honor of Suzan's homegoing, hoping that those who are lost will come to a point of committing their lives to Christ, and those who need to be strengthened in their faith will understand that while Christians do suffer intense pain, the Great Physician can and will use our pain to strengthen us and to make us more effective witnesses for His kingdom.

Words make a big difference in our lives, and my earnest desire is that the words in this book will make a difference in the way you approach grief, benefit from grief, and become healed from your deep sadness and sorrow.

If you are a Christian reading this book, my prayer is that you will know the presence of God as you have never known it before, and that you will commit yourself to an even closer and more intimate daily walk with Jesus Christ—that your trust in and dependence on Him will grow and that your willingness to share His love with others will increase.

If you don't know Christ as your personal Savior or you aren't seeking to follow Him as your Lord, my prayer is that as you read this book, God will speak to you in ways that will make His love clear to you, and that you will seek to establish a relationship with Him.

If you are reading this book because you are not sure whether a loved one who has died is secure in the arms of Christ, I trust you will find in this book a reason to have hope.

This book has been written with many tears and even more prayers. It has been written with the prayers of countless prayer warriors who have prayed that God will take this message and use it to make a difference in your life. It has been written with the hope that you will experience growth in your faith as the result of reading these words.

May God bless you as you read what God has laid upon my heart to write.

2

THE LOSS OF SUZAN—
OUR BELOVED
FIRSTBORN DAUGHTER

W E HAD KNOWN for some time that Suzan was sick, but we had no idea just how sick she was. When she was taken to the hospital on April 28, 1995, we expected her stay to be a temporary one before going on to St. Louis where she would be evaluated for a lung transplant. Her condition, however, deteriorated rapidly.

My son-in-law and Suzan's brother-in-law, Jim Norman, kept a journal during the last fifteen days that we spent at the hospital with Suzan. I have included excerpts from it here at the outset of this book to give you a feeling of what I and my family experienced at the close of my daughter's life on this earth. After Suzan died, so many of our friends and more distant family members asked me, "What happened?" Suzan's illness and death seemed so sudden and unexpected to them. I realized background information related to Suzan's death helped them understand more fully how it was that we in the immediate Ziglar family were responding to her death. I believe you will understand more clearly the reason and the hope expressed later in this book if you also have this foundation of what happened.

Before turning to Jim's diary, let me give you a little background information on our family.

July 4, 1972, was the day I accepted Christ as my Savior. The change in my heart also marked an incredible change for the entire Ziglar family. Virtually all of the success I have known has come about since that date. And since that date, I have seen all of my children commit their lives to Christ.

Prior to that time, the Ziglars were not a spiritually centered family. We were "good people," struggling to make it through life on our own efforts. When I became a Christian, I knew that I was not the center of my life. I realized that all I am and all I have is a gift from God. My perspective on life changed dramatically. I had no greater desire than for each of my children to experience the new relationship I had discovered with my faith in Jesus Christ.

In her early years, Suzan considered herself to be an agnostic. She suffered through years of depression as a young adult, and her spiritual condition concerned my wife and me. In 1978, I wrote *Confessions of a Happy Christian,* and the primary reason I wrote it was for Suzan. Between the first and second printings of that book, both Suzan and her husband, Chad, accepted Christ. She was the last member of our immediate family to come to know the Lord.

In the years that followed Suzan's acceptance of Christ as her Savior, she grew into a tower of faith. All of us in the family witnessed her spiritual growth from year to year. Both before and during her illness, Suzan walked with Christ in a spirit of hope, optimism, and good humor. Although all of us worried and at times expressed our apprehensions about her condition, she was quick to comfort us.

Jim Norman and Suzan had a special relationship in that Jim was six years older than Suzan, making him the oldest of the "children" in our family. She called him Big Old Jim, and when Jim turned fifty, she took it upon herself to sign him up for membership in AARP (American Association of Retired Persons). She officially registered him as Big Old Jim Norman, and although Jim quickly fired off a letter to AARP instructing them to change his name, to this day, he still occasionally receives mail addressed to Big Old Jim Norman. Jim called Suzan BOS (pronounced BOZ), which stood for Big Old Suzie.

Suzan and Jim routinely phoned each other whenever they saw an ad for a geriatric product that they thought the other should know about. One of Jim's favorite tricks was to call Suzan and claim, in a disguised voice, to be taking a survey on some subject, usually one that had to do with aging. Even after Suzan recognized that it was Jim making the call, she would participate in the "survey" with a dry, piercing wit.

In 1990, I was facing some challenges in my company, the Zig Ziglar Corporation, and at Suzan's urging, I called the family together several times that spring to discuss the problems and seek their opinions about possible solutions. It was the first time I had sought business counsel from my family, and one day after several family meetings, Suzan said to me, "Why don't we get Big Old Jim to run the place? I think he can fix things." Jim and I went through several weeks of listening to Suzan badger each of us with the idea that Jim join the company, and in July of 1990, Jim joined the corporation as president and chief executive officer.

At the time Suzan entered the hospital, I was chairman of the board and, then as now, kept a hectic schedule, writing and speaking to more than 250,000 people a year.

Chad Witmeyer, Suzan's husband, was senior vice president of operations.

Tom Ziglar was vice president of sales.

Richard Oates, Cindy's husband, was vice president of marketing and product development.

Suzan was the editor of my nationally syndicated newspaper column, and Julie helped me edit our books.

As you can see, our lives were incredibly mingled. We were bonded together by blood, by marriage, by business and, most significantly, by God. We worked together, played together, and prayed together.

With that as a background, I believe you will have a greater insight into *why* Jim has written some of what he did in his journal. Here, then, is his account of our final days with Suzan.

Friday, May 5, 1995, 3:15 P.M. Suzan Ziglar Witmeyer will be forty-six years old in five days. Today, she is in critical condition in the medical-surgical intensive care unit of St. Paul's Medical Center in Dallas after being transferred by helicopter from Plano HCA Hospital in Plano, Texas, on Monday, May 1. Suzan's family is together in the ICU waiting room.

Suzan is married to Chad Witmeyer, and they are the parents of two daughters, Katherine who is fifteen and Elizabeth who is eleven. Elizabeth contracted a virus in the womb that retarded her mental capabilities; she has required a special mother and father to care for her since birth, and Suzan and Chad have been just that special mother and father she needed.

Suzan is the oldest child of Jean and Hilary Ziglar—Hilary's nickname is "Zig." Zig Ziglar is an internationally known author and motivational speaker. Suzan has two sisters and a brother. Cindy, the "middle daughter," is married to

Richard Oates. Julie, the youngest of the Ziglar girls, is my wife. Tom Ziglar is the "baby" of the family, sixteen years younger than Suzan, although a thirty-year-old man should probably not be referred to as a "baby." Tom is married to Chachis, and they are the proud parents of a new baby daughter, Alexandra.

Today, Suzan is seriously ill, and our family has gathered to wait for whatever God permits to happen. Zig is flying back from Chicago and will be with us in a couple of hours.

A little over a year ago Suzan began to experience shortness of breath and was diagnosed with pulmonary fibrosis. Fibrosis is a progressive condition that eventually is fatal unless the patient has a lung transplant. Last week, Suzan's condition accelerated dramatically, and she was hospitalized. We had believed that she had several years to live before her disease reached a critical point. Something has happened to change that assumption. She has been in a critical condition for several days with congestive heart failure and an inability to absorb oxygen. We worry that she may not be able to survive all of this.

As I write, they have just taken Suzan to a surgery suite to perform an angiogram on her lungs to see if they can find any blood clots. It is a risky procedure because she is very weak.

Friday, May 5, 1995, 11:45 P.M. The doctor reported no blood clots when he met with us at four o'clock. As he was speaking with us, Zig arrived. Finding blood clots would have given the medical professionals something to treat, but as it stands now, the doctors are telling us that Suzan's only hope is a lung transplant and that she will be very fortunate if a donor lung is available in time. We were all stunned by this news. After the doctor left, we spent a considerable amount of time crying together and holding each other.

13

Suzan has O-negative blood, and several family members also have this blood type. They asked the doctor if they could donate a lung for Suzan. The doctor said no. I am struck by the fact that we are now waiting for the death of another to save someone we love so dearly.

Suzan's physician, Dr. Randall L. Rosenblatt, met with us at six o'clock. He gave us a detailed presentation about Suzan's disease, and he eventually reached the purpose of his meeting with us. It is the opinion of the doctors that Suzan would not be able to survive a transplant operation even if a lung became available, and therefore, she is not even going to be considered as a candidate for transplant.

The only medical option available is a long shot. Dr. Rosenblatt intends to administer a massive dose of steroids with the slight chance that the steroids will reduce the lung inflammation and improve her oxygen-transfer ability. He noted candidly that this procedure is almost never effective, but it is the last medical option. He estimates she will live no more than a week and possibly no longer than twenty-four hours.

We have all stepped into the emotional reality of grieving for the impending death of a loved one. The beautiful woman we all love so dearly is about to leave us and step through the door of eternity to be with God who loves all of us so much. We all know the magnificence of the great promise and the incredible inheritance we have been given through Christ. There is no doubt among us that Suzan is moving on to a far superior condition. But it still hurts. We have solid theology in our minds, but there is tremendous pain and an immense sense of loss in our hearts.

After the doctor left we gathered at Suzan's bedside. She is heavily sedated, almost in an induced coma, although the doctors have assured us that she can hear and understand what is going on around her. We clasped hands and tearfully prayed

14

for God's will to be done. We asked Him to comfort us and allow us to feel His loving presence. One of the ICU nurses took our hands and joined with us as we prayed.

After we spent time with Suzan, we began to cluster together in groups of two and three. The theme of each of our conversations was gratitude that Suzie would not experience a lengthy period of suffering. Many of us in the family have been concerned for some time that the possible complications from a lung transplant would put Suzan through years of problems and may ultimately prove to be only a temporary solution. (There is only a 50 percent survival rate in the first five years following a lung transplant.) We also talked about how grateful we are to be a family with faith. We have seen others in waiting rooms during the past week who do not seem to have what we have as a family. The difference is striking, and it is tragic to see people who do not know God experiencing a crisis.

Times like these confirm the fact that death is harder on those who will survive a departing mother, wife, daughter, sister, and friend. A man should not lose his wife at age forty-six. Fifteen- and eleven-year-old girls should not lose their mother so early in their lives. A mother and father should not have to bury their children. But this evidently will happen to us very soon.

The entire medical staff at this hospital is performing like a well-oiled machine. They are all doing their jobs with care and compassion. It is evident that Suzan's nurses are emotionally involved in her case, as well as professionally involved. When Dr. Rosenblatt met with us at six o'clock to give us the grim facts, everybody working in the ICU became quiet, and we could see the pain in their eyes as they watched us receive his news.

One of the things I have heard Zig say often is, "You can have everything in life you want if you will just help enough *other people get what they want." The truth of that saying filled my mind as I watched these wonderful nurses go about their duties.*

I have also been aware that many of the nurses attending Suzan have been exposed to the principles and ideas in our training programs since St. Paul's Medical Center has been a customer of the Zig Ziglar Corporation for the last couple of years. Today, we are reaping a benefit. The ideas that Zig has shared with hundreds of thousands of people for so long have seemingly come full circle for us at this time. The building is full of caring hospital employees who are sensitive to our needs and who are going about their tasks with tenderness and understanding. God is certainly good and specifically honors His promise, "You shall reap what you sow."

One of the things I have thought a great deal about in recent days is how my own father struggled for breath during his last days. I have thought about my smoking habit and have realized that the time may have come for me to give up this habit. Julie quit smoking six months ago. Suzan quit smoking four years ago. Suzan's doctors have assured us that her condition occurs equally in smokers and nonsmokers, but I am fully aware that smoking can produce or contribute to many fatal illnesses. As I said my prayers tonight, I asked God to give me the willingness to quit.

Saturday, May 6, 1995, 6:00 P.M. *About nine o'clock this morning, Julie came home from the hospital. She had been up all night with her mother and sister Cindy. She was very sad, and I wish I could say or do something that might help her through this pain. She, in turn, is concerned about me. I told her that I am at peace, although I am hurting deeply for Chad, his children, and the rest of the family. I faced a medical scare three years ago and, for two weeks, felt certain that I was going* to die of lymphoma. I had every indication of the disease, but the biopsies were benign. Through that experience, I became about as comfortable with the idea of death as a person can get without actually experiencing it. I became very aware that going to be with God would be a wonderful thing. From a self-ish perspective, a person can't hope for a better "condition" than to be with the Lord. I know Suzan feels that same way.

At noon, we received a call from Chachis that Suzan's oxygen transfer numbers are better today than yesterday and the doctor has reduced her medication to allow her to respond to conversations with a yes or no nod of her head. Could it be that the doctor's long-shot, massive steroid dose is going to work? Are we going to experience a miracle? We will pray it is so.

At one o'clock, we received a second call that Suzan is definitely improving, although it is too soon to tell if the improvement is temporary. The doctor has opened a small window of hope. Jean, Zig, and Cindy are with Suzan. They are talking to her, and Suzan is communicating by nodding her head. This is truly an answer to prayer. When Zig returned from Chicago yesterday, Suzan was heavily sedated and unable to communicate. Zig desperately wanted the opportunity to talk to Suzan and to know that she was hearing him. Her sudden improvement has made this possible.

We are aware that literally thousands of people are praying for Suzan and have been praying all last week. There are scores of church congregations interceding daily on her behalf. The sixty people who are part of the Zig Ziglar corporate family have engaged support from their friends, families, and churches to pray for Suzan. Friends of the Ziglar family from around the world have joined in prayer. We will keep praying and try to maintain our hope.

When I arrived at the hospital in the middle of the afternoon, I found an atmosphere of guarded optimism among the *family members. Suzan's oxygen transfer numbers are much better than yesterday's. This is not what the doctor told us to expect.*

Yesterday the medical staff allowed us to be with Suzan anytime we wanted, and today they have returned to their restricted visitation policies. Tom, Richard, and I see this as a favorable indication. When they felt there was no hope, they were not concerned about how many of us were at her bedside at a time. The visitation limitations are a sign to us that they want her to rest so she can regain strength.

I pray we are not experiencing false hope, although a little relief from the total grief we felt yesterday is probably a healthy situation for us. Jean, Cindy, and Julie did not sleep all night and are running on adrenaline at this point. Chad and Katherine slept restlessly in a guest room provided by the hospital. Suzan's improved condition might allow all of us to get some needed rest.

Tom Ziglar and I went in to see Suzan about five o'clock. Her medication has been increased, but she can hear us, although she can't respond. I teased her that I was looking forward to her birthday this coming Wednesday and that I was going to find a particularly obnoxious card for her. I think she tried to laugh.

Our daughter, Amey, went to her senior prom tonight. Julie stayed with her until her date arrived, and she took photos of Amey and her date. Then Julie and I met each other for dinner at a restaurant before Julie went on to the hospital. It was nice to have dinner with Julie—it was the first time we have shared a meal in the last week. Julie has read a great deal about Suzan's disease for some time. She has also taken several college courses in anatomy and physiology, and is up on medical terminology and related medical topics. I shared the sense of optimism I felt about Suzan's improved condition, and Julie said that she also prays we are not experiencing false hope. She believes the true indication of improvement will be seen when they begin to reduce the percentage of pure oxygen Suzan is receiving. Right now a machine is breathing for her. As the medical staff weans her from this, her own lungs will have to do more work. That's when we will really know.

Sunday, May 7, 1995 Suzan's condition remained stable today, and the family spent most of the day together in the waiting room. The atmosphere of hope has increased, and Zig has encouraged us to believe Suzan will survive this. We all want to believe that will be the case, although the medical realities seem very harsh.

Monday, May 8, 1995 While I was at work this morning, I learned from Tom that Suzan's oxygen absorption numbers dropped at six o'clock, but rose again by nine o'clock. The doctor plans to begin weaning her off the respirator today. This will be a critical step.

I have been wrestling with Zig's speaking schedule. He has three events between Thursday and Saturday. Zig and I discussed this at ten o'clock, and Zig told me that he believes he will be able to keep these engagements because he believes everything with Suzan is going to be fine.

After some discussion, we agreed to notify the appropriate people of the possibility that he might have to cancel his appearances. I called the clients and told them what was happening with Suzan. They were all very understanding and wanted Zig to do what he needed to do.

It is tough to balance the need to maintain hope against the practical realities of Suzan's condition. We all want to believe she will recover, but her condition is still very grave— she is about as sick as a person can be and still be alive. There is a great medical chasm left to cross.

The doctor met with the family at 3:30 in the afternoon. He told us that she is better than she was last Friday. He said he was surprised she survived the weekend. At present she is being administered 100 percent oxygen, and he wants to wean her down to 50 percent with no loss in absorption. If that can be accomplished, they will begin an intravenous nutritional treatment designed to build up her strength—with the hope that she may become strong enough to survive a lung transplant operation. That is the best we can hope for at this point.

After the doctor left, Zig, Jean, Richard, and I sat in a small consultation room outside the intensive care unit. Dr. Jack Graham, Zig's pastor, came to sit and pray with us. Zig's voice was full of optimism and enthusiasm as he told Dr. Graham that we had just received good news that Suzan's condition was "appreciably better."

I kept my mouth shut. The doctor never used the phrase "appreciably better." He just said Suzan was better and refused to express an opinion as to how much better. I interpreted his remarks to mean she was not actively dying as she had been on Friday.

I couldn't help but reflect later on Zig's optimism. It is his greatest quality and also a source of heightened disappointment for him when things don't work out the way he believes they will. I am concerned that he is setting himself up for an emotionally crushing time if Suzan's condition begins to deteriorate.

I believe it takes great faith to feel such unrestricted hope, and Zig has great faith. Expressing great hope makes a person vulnerable to increased pain if the hope is not realized. Most of us lack the courage to allow ourselves to be that vulnerable. Clearly, Zig is wired for great hope and I would never try to change that aspect of his character.

Wednesday, May 10, 1995 *Today Suzan is forty-six. Julie and Cindy bought a birthday gift for Suzan yesterday—a beautiful Hummel figurine of two young girls. The older girl is carrying a basket of flowers, and their faces are filled with expressions of excitement and love. When Julie showed me the figurine, she said that the girls represent her and Cindy, taking a basket of flowers to their big sister. Listening to Julie explain the meaning of the sculpture and watching her cry as she spoke just about tore out my heart. The pain of love in a time of crisis is truly excruciating.*

We went in to visit Suzan two by two to wish her a happy birthday. Jean and I went together, and when Jean asked Suzan if she would like to hear Big Old Jim sing "Happy Birthday," Suzan nodded yes. Knowing Suzan as I do, I felt certain she was thinking, Okay, Big Old Jim, hop to it and entertain me! I deserve your full attention, and I will find great humor in your having to sing to a semicomatose person in an ICU ward. Jean and I sang to her together and I could tell Suzan enjoyed our song immensely, even though I called her Big Old Suzie in my rendition of the song.

At many family gatherings, Jean, Suzan, Cindy and Julie sang as part of our "family entertainment." Jean and Suzan were on key—Cindy and Julie were usually way off key. Suzan was the instigator of these musical eruptions, and you never knew when they were likely to begin or end. She sang with great vigor, and especially enjoyed singing with her mother and sisters.

A newspaper column appeared today in the Dallas Morning News. The columnist was lamenting the fact that he had taken a shot at Zig Ziglar the week before when he had written, "This is not some Zig Ziglar, zippity-do-dah brand of manufactured enthusiasm." He was making the point that he was truly optimistic about something with good reason.

Evidently, a friend of his had called him and suggested that he get to know Zig better. The columnist subsequently called Zig, and this morning's column was very touching. He summarized Suzan's condition and obviously had a better understanding of what it is that Zig really says to people. Zig's message is always that life is tough and that talent and preparation are the real keys to success. He's said this for thirty years. But Zig also says that positive thinking and an optimistic attitude will let you do things better than you would have been able to do them with a negative attitude. The columnist ended his piece with the following statement, "You know, it's pretty easy to take a swipe at someone you don't know. But, right now I've got nothing but positive thoughts for Zig Ziglar and his family."

During the interview, Zig also shared Suzan's faith with the columnist. He quoted Zig us saying, "She was very emphatic that we not tell the girls—Katherine and Elizabeth—that God will provide a miracle. We don't know that. She said, 'You tell them God has a plan, that God is sovereign, and that we are secure in our faith.'" That sounded just like Suzie to me!

The newspaper column was a blessing to us. Many people in the Dallas area have responded and left messages of love and concern. Faxes started arriving at the Ziglar Corporation shortly after the morning edition was released, and they have been comforting to all of us. It staggers my mind to think of all the people who are praying for Suzan.

I wish all of the Christian-bashers and cynics who believe all Christians are hypocrites could witness the incredible drawing together of brothers and sisters in Christ who are assisting us with their prayers. There is no unrealistic raving or insane behavior being displayed—just messages that speak of thousands of loving, caring people who want to help us in any way they can. The many people who are praying truly have become a *"priesthood of believers" interceding to God on behalf of a stricken sister.*

Much of this outpouring of love from so many comes as a direct result of Suzan being Jean and Zig's daughter, but the concern for her is very real and personal, and all those who know Suzan personally, love her. For Zig, and I honestly don't think he understands this fully as yet, this huge outpouring of love is a way for thousands of people to thank him. Many of the letters, calls, and faxes are from people who consider Zig to be a personal friend, even though most of them do not know him personally.

At the Zig Ziglar Corporation we routinely receive pounds of letters every day from people all over the world. Some write only to say hello. Others write for advice. Some write long letters spilling their life stories on paper. The vast majority write expressing deep thanks for the difference Zig has made in their lives through his live presentations, books, and tapes. As incredible as it is to me, Zig makes every effort to respond personally to each letter.

After each of his seminars Zig remains after the session to autograph books and chat with those who want to meet him. He has done this for up to four hours after a presentation. Zig is not only my father-in-law, surrogate (replacement) father, mentor, boss, and close friend; he is a phenomenon to me because regardless of his notoriety and the great outpouring of love he receives from people, he has remained one of the most humble men I have ever known. He always says that it's the message, not the messenger, that is important. He never misses an opportunity to comfort personally anyone who needs his counsel. His door is open to every employee at our company, and many seek his advice when they have a personal or spiritual concern. I have seen him spend hours drafting personal letters to total strangers who have written to him for counsel.

It is no wonder to me that each of Jean and Zig's four children has become a compassionate, thoughtful, faith-filled adult.

Wednesday, May 10, 1995, Evening *At four in the afternoon, Suzan's condition was stable, and Zig left to honor his speaking engagements scheduled for Friday and Saturday. We decided that he seems emotionally up to doing these engagements and that he "needs" to go. If Suzan takes a turn for the worse, he will return immediately. Suzan has shown no real improvement for the past three days—she also has shown no decline. She seems to be trapped in something of a limbo state. The hope we began to feel last Saturday is waning a bit. Little or no progress is being made to wean her from the respirator.*

Suzan's friend Lyn Brown came to see her in the hospital today. That was another blessing! Lyn and Suzan used to work together, and during their time of working together, Lyn became a Christian. At the time, Suzan had not yet accepted Christ and she was upset not only that her friend Lyn had become a Christian but that she had seemingly put Suzan on her list to "evangelize." Lyn had experienced one of those lightning-bolt conversions, and she was very serious about her new relationship with God. Suzan became upset with Lyn's efforts to win her to Christ and put some distance between them. After Suzan became a Christian herself, she again drew near to Lyn, who became one of the people who significantly influenced her spiritual growth.

It is amazing to me the way God works in the life of a person. I can look back and recall many people who desired to impact my life spiritually with their testimony of Christ. I ignored them at a conscious level, but the fact of their influence was remembered nonetheless. Most Christians I know have had a similar experience. God loves us so much that He never gives up putting the truth in front of us, and He uses people to do so.

All of us wish we could tell what is going to happen to Suzan. We seem slowly as a family to be returning to the possibility that she will not survive this ordeal. There is a bit of sadness beneath our hope as we all sense things are not going the way we want them to go.

Friday, May 12, 1995, Near Midnight in the Guest Quarters of the Hospital. *The doctor called the family together at six o'clock this evening. It has been exactly one week since we had the first meeting of this type. He clearly explained to us that we are near the end of Suzan's life. We canceled the remainder of Zig's trip, and he was there with us to hear what the doctor said. We began to repeat the vigil of grief that we started last Friday. Our earthly hope has been exhausted.*

For the past two weeks we have been blessed with the almost continual presence of two wonderful pastors—Jim Lewis, Chad and Suzan's pastor at Plano Bible Church, and John West, an associate pastor at Prestonwood Baptist Church. They have been with us through this entire ordeal, comforting us and listening to us. God could not have provided finer men of faith to minister to our needs. Jack Graham, pastor of Prestonwood Baptist, and Michael FinCannon, Suzan's counselor and "personal" pastor, also visited frequently and were a comfort to us all.

It is midnight now but we are all together, waiting. My spirit is drawn to Jean Ziglar tonight. She has been at this hospital around the clock for the past week, by her dying daughter's side every possible moment, loving her and comforting her. Jean's pain is so intense you can almost touch it, although she walks in it with grace and poise. When I have held her, I have felt the depth of her misery and sensed her grief and impending loss. She just keeps telling me how much Suzan loves me. She comforts each of us in the midst of her own agony. I sense she would trade places with Suzan in an instant if that were possible.

O God, why have You given us this cup to drink? I am angry at moments and wish I could somehow crush all pain, sickness, death, and evil in the world! It is then that I remember, God did just that through the death and resurrection of Jesus Christ.

Saturday, May 13, 1995, 9:45 A.M. *At eight-thirty this morning the doctor told us there was only a short time left. We all gathered around Suzan's bed. Jim Lewis read from the Psalms as we wept and waited. Jim prayed for Suzan and our family. Then Jim sang a beautiful hymn. His lone voice rose above Suzan and filled us all. Jim prayed again and we were silent together. God's presence was all over her room. A peaceful light was streaming in from the window behind Suzan's head. We waited.*

Just moments ago, Big Old Suzie stepped through the door of eternity and is now safely in the loving arms of God. We, being still trapped in our biological bodies, remain here until God escorts each of us to a spiritual reunion with Suzan in the future.

After the nurses removed the tubes and medical equipment from Suzan's body, we gathered again around her bed, joining hands and praying one more time. We thanked God for His promises in Christ and released this precious wife, mother, daughter, and sister into His loving care. We thanked Him for His mercy and for the time He allowed us to be with her this past week. We thanked Him for the extra days and the time to adjust to the idea of her leaving us. We prayed for the comfort of Chad, Katherine, and Elizabeth and pledged our support to

*their needs in the future. We asked that each of us be given a
measure of personal grace in her death—that we might grow
spiritually from this experience. We asked that He give us a
renewed sense of purpose and impress our minds with the value
of life and the importance of living as He would have us live.
And then we kissed her good-bye.*

Thursday, May 18, 1995—Two Days After Suzan's Funeral
*The family gathered on Tuesday, May 16, outside the huge
Prestonwood Baptist Church sanctuary to attend Suzan's
funeral service. Suzan's daughter Elizabeth had been escorted
ahead of us by her therapist to say good-bye to her mother.
Elizabeth has loved and clung to her wonderful mother her
entire life.*

*I watched Elizabeth slowly walk down the long aisle and
approach Suzan's casket. Her back was turned to us so I could
not see her face when she saw her mother for the final time.
However, I did see her tilt her head as she gazed at Suzan, and
I saw her reach out to touch her. I wondered how in the world
she would be able to make sense of all of this when we who have
all our mental faculties are having such a difficult time. And
then I remembered God's mercy and grace.*

*Elizabeth did not cry or express fear. She took her seat with
the rest of us and sat quietly through the entire service. I believe
God comforted her in a special way during that service and
gave her a unique understanding. She clearly knows her
mother has departed us for now, but is somehow safe.*

*It will take some time for the experience of Suzan's sudden
departure to sink in for us. And it may take even more time for
us to see how God will turn this tragedy into something positive. Still, there are already some early indications. One of
Suzan's oldest, closest friends came to Suzan's funeral and
accepted Jesus Christ as her personal Savior the next day. She*

had not seen Suzan in many years and was unaware of Suzan's faith. Zig has told us his intentions of writing a new book in the future titled Confessions of a Grieving Christian. *I have quit smoking.*

The mysteries of God and life are infinite. We each wish we could clearly discern the why of events such as these, but we are not given that privilege. We do know with certainty that we have hope as believers in Christ, a hope that those who do not know Christ do not have.

The Scriptures say that the angels rejoice in heaven when a person receives Christ's forgiveness. I know there is a new citizen in heaven who would urge you to do this and to make Jesus Christ your personal Savior if you have not already done so. Big Old Suzie will no doubt sing a hymn for you from heaven—one filled with love and joy if you make a decision to share the faith that carried her into eternity to rest safely in the arms of God.

3

A WAVE
OF EMOTIONS

GRIEF AFFECTS US spiritually, physically, socially, and in every other facet of life—perhaps most obviously and immediately in our emotions. Although grief in itself might be considered an emotion, it is one that readily intermingles with many other emotions—joy, gratitude, happiness, sorrow, disappointment, frustration, and bewilderment. My family and I felt all these emotions—and various combinations of them—almost immediately after Suzan died.

In my experience with grief, I have felt three emotions predominantly: sorrow, love, and joy. I have found that as I have grieved out of the loss I feel and the sorrow in my heart, my grief is also associated with a tremendous and positive feeling of love for the daughter I have entrusted to heaven. The flip side of this sorrow born of love, then, becomes joy at knowing that Suzan is so much better off now than she ever was when she was with us on earth. This mix of emotions is often strange and extreme. But as I have discovered in sharing my experience with others, this mix is neither uncommon nor unnatural.

RECOVERING FROM EMOTIONAL EXHAUSTION

I had not taken off my shoes for more than thirty hours when we went to make funeral arrangements for Suzan. Chad, his parents, Babe and Don Witmeyer, Jean, and I went to the funeral home together to choose the casket, make the burial arrangements, and purchase the burial plot. Unfortunately the man with whom we dealt at the funeral home turned out *not* to be the ideal person for this grieving family to see. He was an incessant talker and told us a number of times that he was "not a salesman." His chatter, combined with my complete exhaustion, created a situation in which I had to leave the room twice for a few moments to regain my sense of balance and composure.

Finally the ordeal of making decisions at the funeral home was over, the choices were made, and we drove home in somewhat of a daze. We entered a round of making phone calls to other members of the family and taking care of the normal aspects of life. Friends and relatives had to be notified, all of the arrangements related to the funeral service at the church needed to be made, and we also needed to receive calls from family and friends who were in town. It was a period of intense confusion and busyness—in all, a very difficult situation when all I personally wanted was to cry myself to sleep.

At 11:00 P.M. on the day of Suzan's death we turned off the telephones because we could not handle any more calls. At 1:30 A.M. the alarm on a clock that we do not usually use sounded, and I thought it was the phone. As the alarm sounded incessantly, I kept wondering in my half-awake, half-asleep exhaustion why the answering machine had not picked up the call, and I got up to answer the phone. By the time I picked up the phone, my wife found the alarm button on the clock and turned it off. I thought the calling party had hung up. Those few minutes of utter confusion only added to my annoyance and fatigue.

Lying in bed after that, half asleep, half awake, half in denial, and half very aware of the enormity of the sad reality we faced, I think I began to hallucinate. I saw Suzan still alive, down at the hospital, wondering why her daddy had not come to get her and wondering whether she really was at the hospital or the funeral home. It was a terrible "waking nightmare" for me and created the most miserable feeling I have ever had in my life. Nothing of the past day made any sense whatsoever to me.

When I realized that I was not going to go back to a deep sleep for a while, I got up and went into my wife's office and opened her Bible, but I could not read it. So I crawled back into bed but could not sleep. I got up to pray, but I couldn't do that either. My mind and my spirit were totally numb.

(One morning sometime later as I was preparing my Sunday school lesson, I came across Psalm 77:4 (TLB) where David prayed, "I cannot sleep until you act. I am too distressed even to pray!"

Those words struck a responsive chord with me. On that sorrow-filled night, that was my exact position. I could not read my Bible. I could not pray. I could not sleep. In many ways, I was emotionally paralyzed, utterly exhausted emotionally and physically. Thinking back upon it now, I realize how much the prayers of the rest of the family and my Christian brothers, sisters, and friends all over the world have meant to us throughout this grieving period. No doubt some of them were praying for me when I could not pray for myself. How marvelous to have the knowledge that many of them continue to pray for us!)

I gave up and went back to bed but struggled for a long time with the image of Suzan's body right after she died. I couldn't seem to get that visual image from my mind. About three o'clock in the morning, I turned on a Bill Gaither videotape in the VCR downstairs, and although a thunderstorm had knocked out the picture, I could hear the beautiful praise and worship songs sung by Vestal Goodman. I lay down on the floor in front of the television set with my back to the glaring light of the fuzzy screen and, quickly and mercifully, went sound asleep listening to God's grace, His love, and His promises. I slept soundly there for nearly two hours and then got up, returned to my bed upstairs, and slept until seven-forty-five.

In the morning I felt considerably better, but was concerned about the hallucinations I had experienced the night before. I called my friend Dr. Paige Patterson, who in many ways was my pastor for a number of years, to talk to him about these images that had flooded my mind. He assured me that such hallucinations were not uncommon for someone who was as physically and emotionally exhausted as I had been, who had lost someone that had been loved so dearly, and who was experiencing excruciating grief. I felt comforted by what he said and knew with a certainty in my heart that God was, indeed, in control.

LIVING IN SLOW MOTION

When the full impact of our loss hit home, it seemed that everything moved in slow motion. It seemed to take forever for anything to happen, for us to say what we wanted to say and to do the things we needed to do. For the Redhead (my affectionate name for my wife) and me, those first few nights after Suzan's death were nights we thought would never end. We were in shock and time stood still.

The Longest Day was a movie that portrayed the invasion of Normandy in World War II—a day on which many lives were lost, much blood was shed, and many life-destroying or life-saving decisions were made. For me, the longest day of my life was May 13, 1995, the day of Suzan's death. That day was the culmination of fifteen highly intense days—the last nine of which were packed with prayer, emotion, and hope that was almost beyond comprehension in its fervor. The days that followed her death were not as intense, but they seemed just as long *for their lack of intensity.* Although we still had great emotion, the hope that had driven us to stay up hour after hour at Suzan's bedside was not there, at least not in the same way. Our ability to pray needed to return. Our hope needed to be refocused on Suzan's life in eternity rather than on the possibility of her sustained life on earth. It was a slow-motion process.

How does one respond to the emotions of sorrow in the midst of love and in the context of exhaustion? Perhaps the first and foremost way is with tears. And believe me, the tears flowed freely and deeply. A river gushed from the depths of our souls.

GOD'S GIFT OF TEARS

Tears are the natural form of release for the still-suppressed feelings of love and gratitude, and also for the reservoir of pain and sorrow we have in our hearts. In many cases, they bring to the surface the feelings that lie deep within so that we can examine and process those feelings. I have no doubt whatsoever that tears are God's gift to us in grief.

According to every expert in the field of grief recovery that I have read or heard, tears are a natural, good, and healthy response to the loss of a loved one. There is no known benefit to stifling tears. In fact, the exact opposite is true. Some negative health conditions have been related to an inability or unwillingness to cry. I certainly hope the experts who recommend crying are correct because if they are not, our entire family has made and continues to make a humongous mistake.

It is my complete conviction that people who suppress their feelings are not working through their grief. They are denying their grief and delaying the healing process. Sometimes an inevitable result of unexpressed grief is that the grief grows more profound and seems to hurt even more. After each outburst of grief and tears, I have a feeling of relief and a sense that I am moving closer to the solution for my grief—not the solution of eliminating the grief entirely, but the solution of making the grief more bearable and of shifting my focus to all of the marvelous things I remember about my loved one. I must say on behalf of tears that I have always felt better for having wept.

FOR WHOM DO WE CRY?

Certainly many of my tears have been shed solely for myself—my sense of loss, pain, and sorrow. Some of the tears, however, have been for others, especially for Chad, Katherine, and Elizabeth, the family Suzan left behind. Each time I saw them in the months that followed Suzan's death, I could see how profoundly affected they were by the loss of their wife and mother.

I have wept tears that Katherine won't have her mother by her side as she graduates from high school and prepares to leave for college, that she didn't have her mother to help her prepare for her first date, that she won't have the help from her mother as she prepares for her wedding day, and that she won't have the counsel and comfort of her mother as she perhaps has children of her own. Katherine is a beautiful young woman, committed to Christ, and she understands that death is part of life. Only time will tell how God will use her mother's death to bless her life and to do His divine work in Chad, her father. I trust God to use all things for their good and to reflect His glory, but at the same time, I feel sorrow that Katherine will not have her mother's presence for as many years as I enjoyed her mother's presence on this earth.

I believe I have a good precedent for shedding tears on behalf of my family members. I believe that is precisely what Jesus was doing when He wept at the grave of Lazarus. (See John 11:35.) Jesus knew that within minutes He would raise Lazarus from the dead, yet He wept. I believe His tears were a sign of His empathy for Mary and Martha over the loss of their brother. They were very close to Him, and He knew how much they loved Lazarus. He wept for all that Lazarus's death had meant to them and to their community of family and friends. He wept for the sorrow that death brings with it, regardless of how strong a person's faith may be.

NOT A SIGN OF WEAKNESS

Tears often seem to be associated with weakness. From my perspective nothing could be farther from the truth. Some people believe it's okay to weep over the loss of a loved one for a few days, but then you should get over it, take control, and refuse to let Satan claim any kind of victory. Scripturally I believe they are in error.

I am astonished and chagrined at the way man has perverted much of life. For a long time, particularly in our society, people held the opinion that "real men" didn't cry, and yet the shortest verse in the Bible declares that "Jesus wept." I believe that verse was put there to show us that the strongest of all men wept, and if He could and did weep, surely we can.

My personal conclusion is that weeping is helpful and even necessary to effectively deal with grief. As you read my personal experiences with tears, I hope you concur to the degree that if you are grieving, you will be freed to weep. Realize that God understands your weeping and that David wept at length before his infant son's death and later at the death of Absalom. Weeping is generally followed by a sense that "everything is going to be okay," that as great as the loss of a loved one is, there still is a loving God who will bring you comfort.

Men and women are different in the way we show our love, our joy, and our grief. Women cry much more frequently than we men do, and they are more open with their tears. That's why it is so shocking to see a brokenhearted man weep. The cries of anguish, the deep-seated sobs, and the shaking and heaving of the body of the brokenhearted man are a testament to the fact that the man who loves deeply will weep deeply. When a man in deep mourning weeps, he weeps from the bottom of his feet to the top of his head. I know that's the way I weep.

Am I embarrassed by my tears? No.

Is God embarrassed by my tears? No.

The psalmist tells us that God does not frown on tears, but loves them, particularly when we shed them in worship and love, and in grieving for the lost and specifically the lost loved one.

The reality is, if we could not cry, if the tear ducts were not there, our eyes would be dry and we would soon be blind—painfully so. Apparently God designed our tear ducts to be used. He tells us that those of us who "sow in tears shall reap in joy" (Ps. 126:5 NKJV). God also tells us that He will make our eyes to become a fountain of tears (Jer. 9:1). Many times in His Word, God tells us that He sees our tears. He knows our hearts, and He responds to the feelings expressed in tears.

The overriding message throughout the Scriptures is that it is not only all right for us to cry, but it is desirable and beneficial in many ways. All of us have felt better once we have had a good cry.

I do not deliberately seek recordings or programs that cause me to shed tears; neither do I avoid them. Situations arise in the natural course of events that evoke tears, and I do not choose to hold back tears when these moments come. I believe it's a very natural thing for a father to mourn the loss of his daughter with tears.

As time goes by, fewer things drive me to tears, and today I can talk about Suzan and her death with considerably less emotion than I felt and exhibited in the early weeks and months after her death. This change does not signify to me that my love for Suzan has subsided, not in the least; rather, it signifies that God, in His mercy, has brought about many other things in my life that demand my attention. My call to serve is greater than ever, and in pursuing the life that God has put before me, I recognize the need to move forward in strength. That strength has been fueled and nourished by the tears shed through the months.

God uses our tears in many ways during our lives, but the even more wonderful news is that one day in the future we will have no cause for tears. The psalmist declared, "For You have delivered my soul from death, my eyes from tears, and my feet from falling" (Ps. 116:8 NKJV). In Revelation 21:4 (NKJV) we read, "God will wipe away every tear from their eyes; there shall be no more death, nor sorrow, nor crying. There shall be no more pain, for the former things have passed away." I take comfort in that last verse, particularly because I know Suzan experiences no sorrow, crying, or pain.

HOW LONG DO TEARS CONTINUE?

One Sunday as the music in our church spoke about our Lord and memories of Suzan rose in my mind, yet again the tears flowed. I asked myself, I wonder how long this will continue? Will there be a day when I can hear these beautiful melodies and not weep for my daughter?

The thought occurred to me that I'm not sure I ever want the tears to end. In many ways, the tears remind me of what the Lord has done for me and my family as well as for millions of other believers.

In my reading about grief, I came across a story about a family that had lost a child forty years ago, and they still, on occasion, wept for the child. That may seem like a very sad fact to some, yet I found comfort in their story. I know that I am not alone in my moments of tears that are a way of saying, "I love you and I miss you, Suzan." My tears are not tears of anger or bitterness, and for that I am grateful. My tears flow solely because I am hurting at the fact that I cannot enjoy the immediate presence of my daughter.

I don't believe parents are ever ready to surrender their children. We know that Suzan has gone to an infinitely better place. Nevertheless, the tears still come, we still weep, and we still mourn. But what comfort there is in God's Word when He said, "Blessed are those who mourn, for they shall be comforted" (Matt. 5:4 NKJV).

As the grieving process progressed for me, I discovered after several months that I was weeping less frequently and with less intensity than I did in the hours and days immediately following Suzan's death. I was grateful for that since I don't know how I could have continued to live had I continued to weep with such depth of pain and emotion as I had immediately after her homegoing.

Do my less frequent and less intense times of weeping mean that I am getting over my grief? No, I don't believe so. I do believe that as the grieving process continued, God gave me a clearer perspective of His goodness, and my greater perception and understanding of God's love, mercy, grace, and tender care of His children have given me increased strength, hope, and courage. God's goodness has been manifested in a very strong and powerful way to me, increasing the love I feel for Suzan but also increasing my assurance and faith that all things are according to God's plan. I have a renewed understanding that God desires, as Suzan no doubt would, that I continue to undertake the commitments and responsibilities on this earth that God has given me, and to do so with even more urgency to minister God's love and presence to others.

We hear tears loudly on this side of heaven. But we don't often take time to contemplate the *cheers* that are even louder on the other side of death's valley.

My experience teaches me that after we have wept until there are no more tears, we are able to hear heaven's cheers. After we have emptied ourselves of the pain and sorrow in our hearts through our tears, we are able to focus fully on the promise of the eternal life our loved one is now enjoying. In the aftermath of tears our hope rises up to fill the part of us that has been cleansed of pain. When that happens, we know we can keep going until the deep pain of grief has subsided, and we begin to be healed and restored to a greater wholeness than we have known before.

4

FACING THE FEARS
OF DEATH

ONE EVENING WE invited the family over to watch a
Cowboys game with us on our big-screen television set. Just
about the only television shows I watch are news programs,
golf matches, and Cowboys games. After the game, we prepared dinner as a family. I cooked the steaks. My family
praises highly the way I cook steaks, and I suspect their
praise is to encourage me to continue to cook them and to
do so more often! We thoroughly enjoyed our time
together as a family.

As we were preparing to eat, Chad turned in his chair to
move Elizabeth's chair closer to his, and in the process, he
strained his back, bringing on considerable and immediate
pain. A few minutes later, he got up and lay down on the
floor to get some relief. When he did so, a look of deep concern came over Katherine's face. She anxiously asked if he
was all right.

My wife related instantly to what Katherine was feeling
and to the depth of her concern. The Redhead's father

died when she was only ten years old, and she vividly
remembers the concern and anxiety she felt if her mother
was even a few minutes late or if she said she was not feeling well. Many of us will lose our parents in the course of
our lifetimes, but few at such a tender age. Katherine was
very close to her mother and seemed to be aware immediately upon Suzan's death that Chad was now the only one
she could rely on for parental security and love.

I was reminded as I watched the Redhead reassure
Katherine that each of us needs almost constant reassurance, reinforcement, and a sense of knowing that our
Savior is with us and that our loved ones who have died are
with Him. Just as little children need frequent hugs and
parental closeness throughout the day, all of us need constant reminders of the Lord's love and presence.

DEATH GIVES RISE TO FEARS

Death inevitably gives rise to some fears, not only in the young
who lose a parent, but in all who experience this loss. We face
perhaps most immediately the fear of the unknown—what
life will be like without this person, and what life is now like
for the person we have lost. Death creates a stormy time for us
emotionally. We feel tossed to and fro in our emotions. And
when the world is unsettled, fear develops.

As part of Paul's description of his trip to Rome during
a fierce storm at sea, we read, "There stood by me this night
an angel of the God to whom I belong and whom I serve,
saying, 'Do not be afraid, Paul; you must be brought before
Caesar; and indeed God has granted you all those who sail
with you.' Therefore take heart, men, for I believe God that
it will be just as it was told me" (Acts 27:23–25 NKJV).

Just as the Lord was with Paul in the midst of the storm and brought him safely through it, so my family and I have had the certainty during our grief that God is not only with us *in* our grief, but He will bring us safely *through* our grief to a time of resolution and joy. What a wonderful comfort it is to know that in all the storms of life, we can count on the presence of our Lord.

Only the Lord's presence can truly calm our fears. Only Christ can say to our hearts, "Peace, be still." Only the Lord can come to us in the storm of our fears and say, "Fear not, I am with you."

In this chapter, I deal with several of the fears that seem associated with death and therefore are part of our grief. I have discovered in my own experience that fear is not associated with just one thing, nor is it of just one type or intensity. At times fear grips us. At times it is a subtle nagging feeling in the spirit. All fears, however, are subject to our faith—and in that, there is good news!

FEAR OF THE DYING PROCESS

Soon after Suzan died, Dr. Paige Patterson gave me an interesting piece of information that helped me through a critical stage in my grieving process. He pointed out that primitive societies handle death much better than modern societies do. Those who live in primitive societies watch, on a regular basis, both the birth and the death of animals and people, and in many cases, birth and death come much closer together in time for these peoples than they do for people in a modern society. He observed that most people in modern societies today have never seen the birth of an animal or an infant. That is certainly true in my case. I witnessed the birth of a kitten many years ago, but I have never seen a baby born. Until I saw Suzan die, I had never seen a person die.

Dr. Patterson stated that in our modern society the medical community, in most cases, moves parents and family members out of the way, and only doctors and nurses are present during either the first or the final moments or hours of life. Thus, few have seen the beginning and even fewer the ending of a human life. Being absent at the time of death can make complete closure of the experience more difficult for the family.

What he said rang true for me. In the 1940s when Suzan was born, mothers often experienced hours of labor because physicians were hesitant to induce birth. The Redhead was in hard labor for many hours before our first daughter arrived. I was not in the delivery room when she was born. I was just outside the room, and I had been there for nearly thirty hours. Both the Redhead and I experienced great physical relief and unspeakable joy at the arrival of our long-awaited daughter.

In the final two weeks of Suzan's life, we spent many hours with Suzan, and we were able to come to grips with the fact that we were going to lose her. During the final twenty-four hours of her life, at least one member of the family was with her at all times. In the last few hours, most of us in her immediate family were with her. I believe this helped in bringing us to the point of closure that she had actually gone on to be with the Lord. We are all grateful for that time we had with her. Some of the fear of not knowing *how* a person passes into eternity is not there for us. Neither do we have fear that dying was painful or a struggle for Suzan.

As we left church just two weeks after Suzan's death, David Brickley told us that he had felt impressed to visit us while Suzan was in the hospital, but had gotten busy and had not followed through on that impression. When he heard that Suzan had died, he was distressed that he had not done what he had felt in his heart was the right thing to do. He went on to tell us that a few months earlier he had experienced a heart attack and had actually died on the operating table. He was careful to say that while he knew some people do not fully comprehend "out of body" experiences, he knew that virtually everybody has heard about them. He was right on both accounts. Then he shared his experience.

He told us that he sensed himself rising above the doctors, and he could see his body lying on the operating table as he looked down. He also watched those who were working on him. He stated that he knew he was dead, but at the same time, he felt peace. He wanted to assure us that death itself is painless, and he felt we would receive a degree of comfort in knowing that as Suzan passed away, she was in neither agony nor pain.

Interestingly enough, the doctors had already assured us of that fact. The room was quiet and peaceful as Suzan slipped away to spend eternity with our Lord. While we had held no thought that Suzan was suffering as she died, we found this man's unique experience to be comforting, and we appreciated his courage and kindness in sharing his experience with us.

If you are fearful today about the pain your loved one might have experienced in dying, I encourage you to believe that the actual moment of passing was one of peace. I hope the following story I heard many years ago will be as helpful to you as it has been to me.

A father's little girl was on her deathbed. The little girl, though young, understood what was happening to her and asked what it was like to die. The heartbroken father paused, prayed for a moment, asking God for the answer, and then said, "Honey, do you remember the number of times we've been visiting in the den on the sofa with your mother, and after a time you would fall asleep there in my arms or lying on the sofa, and the next morning you would awaken in your bed?" The little girl said yes, she remembered that. The father said, "That's what it's like for one of God's children to die. You will simply go to sleep here, and when you awaken, you'll be with Jesus. You'll be in His loving arms, not ours. But His arms are longer and stronger and far more loving than ours could ever be."

FEAR THAT GOD HAS ABANDONED US

Neal Jeffrey, an associate minister at our church, once preached a powerful sermon from Acts 7:55–56 (TLB), which is about the death of Stephen: "Stephen, full of the Holy Spirit, gazed steadily upward into heaven and saw the glory of God and Jesus standing at God's right hand. And he told them, 'Look, I see the heavens opened and Jesus the Messiah standing beside God, at his right hand!'" Acts 7:59–60 (TLB) says, "As the murderous stones came hurtling at him, Stephen prayed, 'Lord Jesus, receive my spirit.' And he fell to his knees, shouting, 'Lord, don't charge them with this sin!' and with that, he died."

Neal pointed out that God's loving-kindness is better than life itself; God loves us just as we are. He spoke of the power of love—no matter whether a mate walks out on you or your friends walk away from you, God will never walk out on you. His love is based not on our holding tightly to Him but on His holding tightly to us through all circumstances and situations.

I heard an interesting story along this line from radio evangelist Steve Brown. Steve was raised in North Carolina near a Cherokee reservation, and the story involves one of their cultural traditions. As a Cherokee youth moved into manhood, the tribe had a custom of taking the young man into the middle of the woods on a dark night and leaving him there by himself. Needless to say, the young man heard every owl hoot, every branch rustled by the breeze, every falling pinecone, and even scurrying rodents. He had no trouble imagining that every shadow was a black bear looking for a meal. It was usually a terror-filled night for the youth, who anxiously awaited the comfort of dawn.

What happened at dawn? As the young Cherokee strained his eyes to see his surroundings more clearly, one of the first things he would see was his father, standing watch nearby, with weapons, ready to protect him. The youth, of course, had no idea that his father had stood guard all night.

Steve points out that this is an excellent picture of God, who stands by us in the darkest, most terror-filled nights, fully prepared to defend us as His children. I like that picture. It perfectly depicts my heavenly Father who watches all that I do, who has been watching me since I was conceived in my mother's womb, and who knew everything about me before the foundations of the earth were set in place. He is the same heavenly Father who was with Suzan throughout her life's journey and who was with her as she stepped into eternity.

When I recently reread the journal that I kept for more than three years after Suzan's death, I was amazed to see how many times I drew comfort from recognizing again and again, "Suzan is with the Lord." I needed to frequently recall that fact to my mind and heart to reinforce my faith that Suzan is with the Lord and that He will never leave her. He is with her and she is with Him, *forever and ever.* Knowing that does not eliminate the grief, but it makes it more bearable to realize that God never abandons us for even a moment of life or death.

THE ANTIDOTE FOR OUR FEARS

My friend Dr. O. S. Hawkins, former pastor of the First Baptist Church of Dallas, preached a beautiful and powerful sermon on Psalm 23 about why the believer should have no fear of death. Let me share with you some of what he said:

> We read in Psalm 23:4 (NKJV), "Yea, though I walk through the valley of the shadow of death, I will fear no evil; for You are with me." David is telling us that God removes the fear of death from us with two things.
>
> First of all, God removes the fear of death from us with true facts. In the first part of this verse, David outlines three things that everybody, and especially believers, ought to know about death. Fact number one is that death is a surety. If Jesus tarries His return beyond our lifetimes, it is a certainty, a surety that we each will die. Death is a surety.
>
> Fact number two is this: death is not only a surety; it is a sojourn. I love how David says, "Yea, though I walk *through* the valley of the shadow of death." He was saying, in effect, "I'm walking toward an appointment." He didn't have a preoccupation with death that caused him to run toward the valley of the shadow, nor was anybody dragging

him toward this valley. Rather, he simply was walking through his life toward that inevitable appointment of going *through* the valley of the shadow of death. Furthermore, this was a temporary passage. He didn't believe that he would get to this valley and reside there. He was journeying through the valley to the other side.

Fact number three is this: death is a shadow. That's all it is. David said, "Yea, though I walk through the valley of the *shadow* of death." Shadows can sometimes frighten us, but shadows cannot hurt us. Shadows have no real substance. I can't walk through the pulpit from which I speak. But when I see the shadow of the pulpit that is cast by the television lights, I *can* walk right through that shadow without harm or hindrance. So it is with death.

God removes the fear of death from us when we face these true facts about death. Facts help alleviate fear no matter what the fear is about. Many people are afraid of things simply because they are unknown and they have never studied the real facts regarding them. For the believer, death is a walk-through and a shadow, even as it is a certainty.

Second, God removes the fear of death from us not only with true facts but with true faith. When you couple true faith in Jesus Christ, with the true facts of God's Word, two things will happen to you. First of all, true faith will remove your fears. David says in the next phrase of this verse, "I will fear no evil." Second, true faith establishes your fellowship with God. As David says in faith, "For You [God] are with me."

David is not denying that fear is associated with the valley of the shadow of death. Rather, he is saying, "I will fear *no evil* associated with this shadow." Fear has a paralyzing effect on us and it strangles our joy. What causes us *not* to feel this fear? When we recognize that the Lord is with us. When we know with a certainty born of faith that we are not alone in going through the valley of the shadow of death, fear is removed from us. We move through this valley in the *love* of God rather than the fear of evil.

In 1 John 4:18 (NKJV) we read, "Perfect love casts out fear." Believers in Christ have no fear of death because they are experiencing the perfect love of Jesus Christ. As the apostle Paul wrote to Timothy, God does not give us the spirit of fear, but of power and of love and of a sound mind. God replaces for the believer the fear of evil with His own presence: love, power, and a sound mind.

Solomon tells us in Proverbs 3:7–8 (NKJV), "Do not be wise in your own eyes; fear the LORD and depart from evil. It will be health to your flesh, and strength to your bones." The fear of death flees when we face death with true facts and with true faith coupled together. At the moment you find yourself facing death, none of the New Age philosophies, positive mental attitudes, or numerous "success" habits are going to do you any good. True faith is what will alleviate your fear.

Paul wrote in 1 Corinthians 15, "Death is swallowed up in victory. It has lost its sting." (See 1 Cor. 15:54–55.) If you are a Christian, there is no sting in death for you. It's like a bee that stings once and then is rendered harmless because it loses its stinger when it stings that one time. Jesus Christ went to the cross, and He took the stinger of the bee of death for you and me. Death no longer has a "sting" to inflict on us.

One of my favorite stories is about a little boy and his dad who were riding in a car when suddenly the little boy screamed, "Daddy, there's a bee in here!" He screamed in terror because a bee sting had nearly killed him on an earlier occasion and the doctor had warned him and his family that another sting could be fatal. The father saw the bee, reached over, and grabbed it in his hand, and then a moment later, he released the bee. The little boy screamed again, "Daddy, he might sting me!" The father looked at his little boy and said, "No, son, he stung me and I took the only stinger he had."

The disciples faced death without fear. They knew they would pass through the shadow of death to join with Christ on the other side of the valley. That's what enabled them not to experience fear. They knew that He was with them in the valley and that they would emerge from the valley with Him, ever more to live with Him. It was with this confidence that they died martyrs' deaths—burned at the stake, crucified upside down, stoned to death, beheaded, thrown to lions. The first Christians were absolutely convinced that even though one might kill the body, one could never kill the soul. Their faith removed fear of death from them, and that is what genuine faith will do.

True faith not only removes fears, but it restores our fellowship with God. David said, "I will fear no evil; *for You are with me.*" King David's friends failed him. Some of his family members had threatened his life. But as death approached, he had a calm assurance because he knew with certainty that he was not alone. Remember that David was a ruddy-faced shepherd boy, tending the sheep of his father in the fields near Bethlehem, when the prophet Samuel came to anoint him king. As a shepherd he knew that sheep never go through a valley alone, that the shepherd is always with them. This was his hope all his life and as he faced death: "The LORD is my shepherd." It is that hope that builds the faith that drives away all fear.

Before Christ ascended back to heaven, He said to His followers on the Mount of Olives, "I will be with you always." Those are words that we must allow to build hope in us. The Lord said in Isaiah 41, "Fear not, for I am with you; be not dismayed, for I am your God. I will strengthen you, yes, I will help you, I will uphold you with My righteous right hand" (v. 10 NKJV).

Throughout Psalm 23 David places his emphasis on the Lord. *The Lord* is his shepherd. *He* makes David to lie down in green pastures. *He* leads David beside still waters. *He* restores David's soul. *He* leads David in paths of righteousness. *He* accompanies David through the valley of the shadow of death.

What the Lord did for David, He does for us. He is present with us always, in every moment of our lives committed to Him, and in every step of our journey through the valley of the shadow.

What a tremendous faith-building message that was to me! Truly my awareness that Christ is *with me always*—that He is with me right now in my grief and in my life on this earth, just as much as He is with Suzan in her joy and in her life in heaven—drives away my fear.

Are you struggling with fears in the aftermath of a loss?

I encourage you to do what the words of an old gospel song advise:

> Turn your eyes upon Jesus,
> Look full in His wonderful face,
> And the things of earth will grow strangely dim
> In the light of His glory and grace.

Jesus is the solution, the answer, the calm for our fears.

5

THE DIFFERENCE
CHRIST MAKES

I TRULY DO NOT know how people without Christ, or without the certainty that a loved one knew Christ, can handle the pain of grief. It is true that all of us can cling to some measure of hope if we know Christ and yet are not sure about a loved one's spiritual state, because we never know fully the state of a person's spiritual life when he enters eternity. There is always the hope that the person might have accepted Christ during the last moments of his life.

For the parent who loses an infant or a small child who has not reached the age of accountability, including a mentally retarded individual, you can rest assured that a loving God takes the child home to be with Him.

My family had peace of mind because Suzan believed in the Lord Jesus Christ as her Savior, and she lived her life with the expressed purpose of worshiping and loving the Lord. My family is able to walk, talk, and sleep with the complete assurance, based upon God's Word and its promises of eternal life, that Suzan is with the Lord and that we will spend eternity with the Lord and with her.

Does Christ make a difference? One of our close family friends, who spent much time with us at the hospital and funeral home and who attended Suzan's funeral service, suddenly found herself called upon to be with the family of some relatives who had lost a loved one almost immediately after her experience with us. She was overwhelmed by the differences she saw in the way the two families handled their losses.

Our friend said that at the other funeral she attended, the family members were arguing, displaying temper tantrums and selfishness, and making evident a feeling of estrangement among them. There was no mention of Christ in their midst. There was no sense of hope that their loved one was with Christ and experiencing glorious joy in heaven.

I cannot imagine the pain of being in such a state after the death of a loved one.

Our family has drawn even closer together, if that is possible, in the aftermath of Suzan's death. The love and support each member of the family has given to all other members of the family have been very important to us. We have been able to express our grief and our love for Suzan openly and unreservedly. The commitments we have made to one another following her death have bound us even tighter together in familial and Christian love. Since Suzan's death, we have spent even more time together as a family.

BECAUSE OF CHRIST, WE HAVE LIFE!

Suzan is alive today solely because of Christ. I believe that to the very core of my being.

Three days after the funeral, the lyrics of one of the songs that Rick Brisco had sung so beautifully at the service, "Because He Lives," echoed through my mind, and I caught a glimmer of the hope that would sustain me and continue to grow in me throughout the next few years as I went through the grieving process for my daughter. Because Jesus lives, Suzan continues to live with Him. And because Suzan lives, I have the assurance that I will be with her again. I have a strong conviction that her life is more full and more joyful than it ever was on this earth—even though she had a great capacity for joy, exuberance, and excitement. I have total faith that we will live together in joy forever.

Christ gives us life; furthermore, He *is* life. Wherever He is, we find vibrant, eternal, abundant life. He said of Himself, "I am the way, the truth, and the life" (John 14:6 NKJV).

The apostle Paul said that for a Christian to be absent from this life is to be present with the Lord (2 Cor. 5:8). To be present with Him is to experience His life, His fellowship, His eternal glory!

BECAUSE OF CHRIST, SUZAN HAS
A HEAVENLY HOME

At the funeral of the beloved gospel singer Janice Mossima, one of those who spoke a eulogy for her said, "We didn't *lose* Janice because we know where she is, and how can you lose anything when you know where it is?" Yes, we lost Suzan's presence and we will always miss her, but we know where she is and we know that we will see her again.

The assurance that we have of Suzan's life and her presence in heaven with Christ is directly related to one thing, and to one thing alone—Suzan's confession of Christ as her Savior and Lord.

"THANK YOU, DADDY"

"Thank you, Daddy."

Those were the words with which Suzan greeted me as we met in the hotel where I had just finished speaking. Suzan hugged me and kissed me and said, "Thank you, Daddy, for finding Jesus seven years ago, because if you hadn't found Him then, I wouldn't know Him now." I did what all Christian brothers and sisters tend to do in such a moment. I hugged and kissed Suzan and cried a little. Then I did what a loving father does in moments like that—I hugged and kissed her again and shed a few more tears.

When I committed my life to Christ on July 4, 1972, I found such joy and peace and excitement that I immediately wanted everyone in the world and especially those God had entrusted to my care to experience what I had experienced. One by one, my children came into the fold of Christ's love and forgiveness and experienced the joy of the Lord. Suzan, however, did not open her heart to salvation. My heart ached that my oldest daughter, my firstborn child, did not know Jesus.

As I have said previously, I wrote *Confessions of a Happy Christian* expressly for Suzan. Every word, every phrase, every sentence, every thought, every paragraph in the first printing of that book was for her.

Finally the long-awaited day arrived when the book was in the hands of the publisher. After what seemed like an eternity, we received our copies of the printed book, and I immediately gave a copy to each member of my family.

They all started reading it with eagerness, except for Suzan and Chad, whom Suzan had married while I was writing the book.

Patience, Dad, patience. How many times did that thought come to my mind! Undoubtedly the toughest assignment I had ever self-imposed was the assignment of *not* asking Suzan and Chad if they had read the book. I had a deep sense that I was not to push them to read it. Anxiously I waited as the days stretched into weeks.

Then Suzan and Chad became involved with a direct sales company under the leadership of a godly couple who had all the qualities one tends to find in genuinely success-ful people. They were successful in their spiritual lives as well as in their family and business lives. They were loving and caring, and they had a large number of associates who were cut from the same bolt of cloth. In that working envi-ronment, Suzan and Chad were inspired to explore good literature and also to attend church. But still, they had not read *Confessions of a Happy Christian.*

Then one night it happened. Suzan opened the book and began to read. She called me, and the enthusiasm in her voice was unmistakable as she described her feelings while reading the book. She told me she had never seen so much joy and happiness jump off the pages of any book. I breathed a prayer of thanksgiving and knew that the Lord's timing was perfect. He was right on schedule, even though His schedule might not have been mine!

After a couple of weeks and a few visits with Suzan and Chad, the two of them came to our home one Sunday after-noon. I felt strongly that God's Spirit was moving, and they were ready to commit their lives to Christ. After carefully and prayerfully leading them through what I believed were the necessary preliminary steps, I asked them if they were ready to accept Jesus Christ as their Savior and to commit their lives to Him as their Lord. Chad responded that he felt he had already taken this step. His response thrilled me tremendously not only because of our love and concern for Chad personally, but also because I was hopeful that his commitment and leadership would encourage Suzan to take the same step. Yet when I asked Suzan if she was ready to make this step of faith and commitment, she responded in the negative.

I was stunned, heartbroken, and deeply disappointed by her answer. I had learned, however, that when you leave things up to the Lord, He brings about His results in His own way and in His own timing. Even so, I must confess that I know also that when the Holy Spirit beckons us and we decline His invitation to come to Christ, there is no assurance that He will beckon us again in the near future. I was distressed at Suzan's reluctance to make her commitment when it seemed so obvious to me that the Holy Spirit was wooing her to Christ.

Eight days later, after much prayer asking God to claim Suzan for His very own, she made her commitment. You can imagine the feeling of total exhilaration I felt when Suzan personally gave me the good news that she had accepted Jesus Christ as her Savior and had made a commitment to serving Him as her Lord!

With a light step and a grateful heart, I walked downstairs with Suzan to meet Chad and Tom in the restaurant of the hotel for a snack. When Tom sat down, I looked at him and said, "Son, guess who Suzan just met." A fleeting stunned expression crossed his face, then his eyes filled with tears, and he bowed his head and wept.

When Tom and I returned home later that evening and walked into the entrance hall, we saw the Redhead standing on the other side of the den. Before either of us could say anything, she spoke up and said, "Suzan knows the Lord, doesn't she?" I responded, "Yes, she does. She's safe." The three of us embraced and wept the tears of joy that expressed our delight, and yes, relief, that we knew our Suzan was safe and her eternity was secure.

A DESIRE TO SHARE CHRIST

Knowing that Christ is the *reason* for our great hope and assurance that Suzan is alive forever and in the presence of the Lord compels me—and, I believe, everyone who truly believes this—to want others to have that hope and assurance.

Evangelist Rodney Gage once spoke at our church and told a story that was personally very painful for him. Soon after Rodney committed his life to Christ, he spent several hours with a lifelong friend but failed to witness to him about Christ. Later that night his friend was killed. As Rodney shared his story with us, I felt pain for him, but I also felt a gratitude that God had compelled me to write *Confessions of a Happy Christian.* And I felt a renewed desire that others might come to a saving knowledge of Jesus Christ and make a deeper commitment to serving Him as Lord. I deeply desire others to know what Suzan knows today—the exuberance and security of being safe in the arms of Jesus!

Our pastor, Jack Graham, said in a sermon that "sorrow is the soil in which the flower of faith grows." It is so true in my experience of grieving. Christ has been faithful, and my faith has grown in the aftermath of Suzan's death. I feel more of the Lord's presence and power, and my faith and my motivation to win souls for Christ are stronger than ever.

Dr. Graham said, "Faith is taking God at His word, and when we do, we enjoy the consequences of faith." Those consequences are spelled out in John 4:53 (NKJV), which says, "So the father knew that it was at the same hour in which Jesus said to him, 'Your son lives.' And he himself believed, and his whole household." This is the end of the story about a Roman nobleman who had come to Christ, asking Him to heal his son. Christ had simply said to him, "Go your way; your son lives." The next day, when the man returned home, he was told that the fever had left his son at the exact hour when Christ had spoken those words to him. The consequences of our faith are that when we believe in and trust Christ, our entire household comes to know Christ. The spiritual renewal in the family was a significantly greater miracle than the fact that Christ had healed the man's son. Spiritual salvation is not behavior modification. It is life modification. It is life saving and life enriching. And it is our *only* genuine balm for grief.

One of the people who attended Suzan's funeral was Shirley Christi, who lived with our family for more than a year. She and Suzan had shared a cynicism—at least a skepticism with perhaps a little disdain thrown in—about "religion." Shirley flew in from Portland, Oregon, to attend the service, and it became obvious to her, as she listened to the comments made, witnessed the tears shed, and watched our family and close friends give testimony to Suzan's great faith, that something significant had happened in Suzan's life since the time she had last seen Suzan.

I sat down with Shirley and shared with her my conversion experience. I told her that my love for my wife and children grew dramatically when I learned to love them through Christ, that I dealt with them in an entirely differ-ent way—becoming far less self-centered and far more fam-ily- and other-people-centered. With tears in her eyes, she said, "I've seen a dramatic difference in you."

I then opened my Bible and shared with Shirley what was required for a person to gain entrance into the king-dom of God. She seemed puzzled and confused by what I said. She admitted she hadn't been in a church in many years. I asked her what she thought was required for a per-son to be given entrance into heaven and to have eternal life, and she had no answer that even bordered on reality. When I asked her if she wanted to be absolutely certain that she would spend eternity with Christ, she quietly responded with a yes. I then started with Ephesians 2:8–9 and read God's Word to her. Then I turned to Romans 10:9, and finally I read John 6:29 to her. These verses are given below:

For by grace you have been saved through faith, and that not of yourselves; it is the gift of God, not of works, lest anyone should boast. (Eph. 2:8–9 NKJV)

If you confess with your mouth the Lord Jesus and believe in your heart that God has raised Him from the dead, you will be saved. (Rom. 10:9 NKJV)

Jesus answered and said to them, "This is the work of God, that you believe in Him whom He sent." (John 6:29 NKJV)

I explained to Shirley that there was nothing she could do that would make her "good enough" to get into heaven, and that there was nothing she could do that was bad enough to keep her out of heaven if she believed in Jesus. I then shared with her John 14:6 (NKJV), which gives us these words of Jesus: "I am the way, the truth, and the life. No one comes to the Father except through Me." Our entrance to heaven is based not on what we do, but on what Jesus did. His shed blood cleanses our sin.

Shirley bowed her head, and together we prayed the sinner's prayer and I am convinced, based on God's Word, that she is safely in the kingdom of God.

After my conversation with Shirley, I called Chad, and my daughter Cindy, who was visiting him and his girls, answered the phone. We chatted a moment, and I told her of Shirley's acceptance of Christ as her Savior. She had been repeating enough of my words so that Chad, who was near the phone, clearly understood what was happening. Cindy said to me, "Dad, Chad just gave us that fist in the air that says *yes!*" He was both excited and grateful at the decision in Shirley's life. With a sob in his voice, he said, "It's already been a great day."

Certainly Shirley's conversion did not lessen Chad's personal grief, but it did help Chad to understand that God's purposes and plans are beyond our understanding in many ways, and that God really does work all things together for good. The only reason Shirley was in Dallas that day was to attend Suzan's funeral. Even in the midst of sorrow, God used Suzan's death as a catalyst to bring yet another soul into His kingdom.

Let me ask you today, Do you know Christ? Have you accepted Him as *your* Savior? Have you truly made a commitment to following Him and serving Him as the Lord of your life? If not, I encourage you to make that decision today. Eternal life and a blessed hope and assurance can be yours. I believe you will discover what my family and I know to be true: Christ not only makes all the difference in this world, but He also makes all the difference in the world to come!

6

FACING THE *WHY* QUESTIONS

W‌HY?"

Countless people ask this question of God in the aftermath of a loved one's death.

"Why did this happen to me?"

"Why was my child taken?"

"Why did this productive adult with three small children lose his life with so much at stake and so much to look forward to?"

I am truly grateful that our faith enables us to move past this question to the point that we no longer feel we have to ask the question or attempt to answer it. We can know by our faith that God has a plan and a purpose, and we can trust Him with that better plan, even if we do not understand it. Getting to that point of faith, however, is not automatic. Most people do have to face and deal with *why* questions.

GOD CAN HANDLE OUR ASKING!

We need to understand that at the time of intense pain brought about by the loss of a loved one, it is natural for little seeds of doubt about our faith to creep into our minds and hearts. God understands this need. God also desires for you to bring any doubts and fears to Him. He wants you to talk to Him about these emotions and read what He has to say about them in His Book. Until you face these emotions in God's presence, you will not be able to reaffirm your faith completely and accept His grace.

The tragedy of losing a loved one sometimes turns feelings of grief into feelings of anger—anger with God for having taken the loved one.

We Christians have the comfort of knowing that God did not "take" our loved one. I believe Suzan's time to be with the Lord had come. It had been foreordained. God knew the day He was going to call her home before she was even born. The Bible tells us that God does not take the death of a loved one lightly. Actually His heart is the first of all hearts to break because He knows the pain that will come to the friends and family of the departed one. No, God did not take your loved one, as we know He did not take Suzan. Rather, He called her to His heavenly home, and just as He shared in the joys of her life, He now shares in the even greater joys at her presence with Him. Just as the Lord shared in the joys that we knew in our relationship with Suzan on this earth, He shares in the pain that we experience in the aftermath of her death.

God's motive toward us—not only in every moment of our lives but also in death—is *love*. Love is His very nature, His character, His temperament, His reason for all action.

It is out of His love that He creates us and plans our lives. It is by His love that He fulfills each person's purpose and reason for being.

As a Christian, I believe Psalm 139:16 (NLT) as never before: "You saw me before I was born. Every day of my life was recorded in your book. Every moment was laid out before a single day had passed." The concept is that God has a departure date for us. He knows the exact time we will enter eternity.

You can do many things to increase the quality of your life, but the time of your earthly departure is not yours to determine. When that moment comes, God will not be the least bit surprised. It is part of His plan for you. Let me encourage you to consider that fact, especially if you are wondering whether there is anything you could have done to prolong your loved one's life or if you are feeling guilty that you were in some way neglectful or that you contributed to your loved one's death.

My belief in Psalm 139:16 removes any feelings of guilt as far as Suzan's death is concerned. We loved her as much as any parents can love their child, and we repeatedly expressed that love to her. We provided her with the best medical care available. We prayed without ceasing that God's will would be done, but our fervent hope was that God would work a miracle and return our Suzan to vibrant health. We did everything we could to keep her with us as long as possible. But in the end, God had ordained the number of her days.

As I reflect on our loss, I realize that as much as we loved Suzan, God loves her more. She is His child, and a loving God would not trust His child's eternal well-being even to parents who deeply loved her. Our faith assures us that God said no to our prayers for her life on earth so He could completely heal her and give her the eternal reward He promised to those who believe. God is good.

When we accept this fact about God's sovereignty and God's providence, we will find ourselves relieved of any responsibility we may have placed on ourselves regarding a loved one's death. As far as I know, not once has any member of our family asked the questions or made the statements, "Maybe we should have . . . ," or "If only . . . ," or "Why didn't we . . . ?" or "Maybe we could have . . ."

To know that God is in control of the number of our days gives us an *assurance* and a hope, even though we may not receive *information* or a reason. Given the option of having assurance or information, I'll take assurance anytime! With assurance, I can trust God with the information.

Ron Ezinga, a brother in the Lord who also was president of our company for ten years, once shared with me that he and his family had been in prayer for a family whose two-year-old son had been run over by a car and killed. He said to me at the time of Suzan's death, "Now, Suzan has gone home to be with the Lord at age 46. Just yesterday our church ministered to a woman who was 106 years old." Somewhere, as Ron put it, there is a thread woven through each of these lives that is difficult, perhaps impossible, to understand. It is a thread of mystery regarding God's timing.

God may choose, in other words, to keep information or reasons from us. But He never withholds His assurance!

GOD DOES NOT PERCEIVE TIME
THE WAY WE DO

One of the things that I have contemplated since Suzan died is this: Why *at this particular time in her life did God choose to call her home?* Perhaps more than wonder about the timing in Suzan's life, I have wondered about the timing in the lives of her daughters.

Suzan will never see Katherine marry or hold her grandchildren in her arms. She will miss Elizabeth's victories and milestones. Those thoughts have been heartbreaking to us.

I feel certain that we are not alone in our asking "Why now?" at what seems to us to be an untimely death. This is no doubt true in all instances of deaths of children or young adults. We ask, "Why did God choose to call this particular one home at this particular time?"

I sometimes ponder just where Suzan would have gone in her life's race had she been allowed to run it longer.

A delight of my life—as bittersweet and ironic as it is— is that just a few months prior to her death, Suzan told me that for the first time, she was experiencing much of the joy I'd been privileged to experience for so many years. She said, "You know, Dad, I'm good at what I do." And was she ever! She added, "I feel so fulfilled, loving what I do and knowing that I am making a difference in others' lives."

Just a few months before Suzan's death, she had started working with me on my daily newspaper column. I found her to be of tremendous help. She had an expansive vocabulary but, more important, a sensitivity toward language and an empathetic compassion and spirit that rounded off the rough edges that sometimes appear in my writing, especially when I feel very strongly about an issue. I praised her constantly for the contributions she made to me in the preparation of our column, and she once said to me, "Dad, I look forward to every column."

I have no doubt that Suzan had genuine writing ability. I saw this repeatedly in her taking charge of our company publication, *Top Performance.* I strongly believe that had she lived longer, Suzan would have been writing her own books and perhaps would have had her own newspaper column. She had the knowledge, the heart, the ability, and the insights to do so. Her death brought about a void in our lives because a certain part of Suzan's potential, from our perspective, never came to full fruition.

How do I find consolation in the face of that fact and feeling?

God does not see time the way we see time. God measures one's success not in terms of longevity but rather as fulfillment of one's God-given purpose in life.

Ultimately Suzan's goal or objective in life was heaven. It had been her goal from the time she committed her life to Christ. And the truth is, Suzan has reached her goal!

November 27, 1996, was a day I will never forget. We attended the funeral services of R. C. and Joan Cook, members of Prestonwood Baptist Church. Friends from seemingly everywhere joined a large number of family members. The service was absolutely beautiful.

During the eulogy, R. C.'s brother, the Reverend Harold Cook, gave the best definition of success I've ever heard. He said, "Success is finishing what God gave you to do." He then elaborated on all that R. C. and Joan had finished. Dr. Jack Graham preached the funeral message entitled "Together and Triumphant." R. C. and Joan had been killed instantly in an accident and went together to be with the Lord "in the twinkling of an eye," which is just the way R. C. had told his son Richard that he hoped to go home to heaven. I couldn't help thinking, *From the world's viewpoint, this was a great tragedy. But as Dr. Graham pointed out so well, from the divine perspective, this was an incredible triumph.* Joan and R. C. had lived together for twenty-three wonderful years, and now in death they were together forever, each of them having finished well the appointed tasks they had been given to do by the Lord.

God is the author of all the seasons of our lives. He is in charge of not only the seasons that we see as being fruitful, productive, and positive, but also the seasons that we human beings tend to see as negatives. He is in charge of the complete rhythm of life. He is Lord over all the seasons!

So often, we focus our attention only on one phase of a loved one's life. To do so is to miss the greater whole.

If we concentrate solely on a loved one's pain and suffering, the physical appearance as the result of an accident or wasting disease, or the loss of function, we will continue to live in a nightmare of gruesome and sad memories. It is wiser and grief relieving to put this period of the person's life into the perspective of his entire life. Although this season might have lasted for days, weeks, months, or even years, it was only a *season* of his life. I encourage you to bring up memories that are from seasons in which the loved one's health, appearance, mental state, and emotional state were good, even superior! Recall the person when he lived with vitality, energy, laughter, loving actions toward others, and ongoing praise and worship of the Lord. Concentrate on the good times, the family jokes and moments of merriment, and the sweet memories of times spent together. Choose to be encouraged that most of the seasons of a loved one's life were very likely good seasons.

And if your loved one never experienced any of the above, take comfort in the fact that he now has a glorified body and will enjoy perfect health, total peace, and absolute joy throughout eternity. All that the loved one experienced in this life was experienced in only a fleeting moment against the unending panorama of heaven. Against the length of eternity, our time spent on this earth cannot even be mathematically calculated. This forever season of a loved one's life so far overshadows even his best seasons of life on earth that they cannot be compared.

If our departed ones could come back to us and tell us about their experiences with the Lord in heaven, I feel certain they would tell us three things. First, they would tell us to concentrate on the way they were when they were at their best in this life. Second, they would tell us to enjoy our lives to the fullest and choose to fill them with the best memories and experiences possible. Third, they would tell us to spend more time getting to know Christ better.

This approach is not denying the reality or even the benefit of grief, but it is putting the focus on a person's whole life. While we can do nothing to bring back a loved one, we can bring to our minds and hearts the fond memories of happy occasions so that we can continue to produce more such memories for ourselves and our other loved ones who still walk this earth with us.

Over the years, I have heard and used a number of expressions that refer to the "dark" or "down" times in life. Among them is the phrase, "It is always darkest just before dawn." Another one is, "The darkest night since the beginning of time did not turn out a single star." Longfellow said, "The lowest ebb is the turn of the tide." Yet another favorite is, "After every sunset we know there is going to be a sunrise." As the sun was setting on Suzan's life here on earth, it was rising in our Savior's home. Suzan instantly experienced the sunrise as she moved into the dawn of eternity.

GOD KNOWS ALL THE PURPOSES
FOR OUR LIVES

A third thing I have learned is this: *God has purposes for our lives that we may not know this side of eternity.* He alone knows all of the purposes for which He created us. He alone knows when those purposes have been fulfilled.

In one of his Sunday school lessons, Associate Pastor Neal Jeffrey told the story of a fifty-three-year-old godly man, beloved by his family, who served the Lord with love, affection, and effectiveness. This man was smitten by cancer, and Neal visited him in the hospital. They were very close as friends, and this man raised the "Why me?" and "Why now?" questions to Neal, pointing out that he had been a good and faithful servant who loved his family and his Lord. There was still much he wanted to do, and he didn't feel that his work for the Lord was finished. He was struggling to understand God's timing.

Neal initially did not know what to say. *Why* is a very difficult question to answer, and it is not a question that often has answers prior to our seeing the Lord Himself. But, as Neal put it, he received a burst of inspiration, and he cautiously said to his friend, "I'm not certain that I have the answer or that anyone else does. It could be that God has called you and chosen you for this. You have shown your family how to live for Christ. Perhaps the Lord now desires that you show your son how a godly man faces his Master."

Neal said that his friend pondered this answer, recognized much truth in it and, from that point on, did not ask the question again. Instead, he did everything in his power to be the kind of man his son and others would look to in faith. He wanted others to see in him a man who had the

71

blessed assurance that when he took his last breath on this earth, his next breath would be in the presence of our Lord. Neal said it was a glorious transformation in this man. At the end of his life, when everyone knew that he had only a matter of minutes left to live on earth, a number of people gathered in his room, including nurses and two of the surgeons who had treated him. The glory of God radiated throughout that room. It was evident to all that he had shown others how to die in Christ. His son testified that one of the greatest lessons he had learned from his dad was how a godly man both lives *and* dies.

To the best of our ability, her mother and I taught Suzan how to live, and she certainly taught us and many others how to glorify Him in our homegoing. That may well have been one of God's foremost purposes for Suzan's life—that she teach others how to live fully and how to die in Christ.

My pastor, Dr. Jack Graham, made an observation that has given me additional hope and encouragement. In recounting the story of Stephen, who prayed for his executioners even as they were stoning him to death, Dr. Graham pointed out that he believed one of the reasons for the stoning and martyrdom of Stephen was the presence of a young zealot named Saul of Tarsus in the crowd. Saul was watching and even urging on those who were casting stones. Saul was a witness to the angelic expression that came on Stephen's face as he was dying. Saul had a fanatical hatred for Christians at that point and was committed to doing everything in his power to eradicate them from the face of the earth. However, as Saul watched Stephen, a beautiful Christian, die, he saw something that had a lasting impact on him.

Try as he might, in Dr. Graham's opinion, Saul could not shake that image from his mind. Not long after that,

God struck Saul blind as he was walking on the road to Damascus. God performed major surgery on Saul and gave him a new heart. He became Paul, an apostle of Christ who was just as zealous and committed to furthering the cause of Christ as he had once been intent upon destroying it.

We have no way of knowing who Suzan might have influenced for Christ—either through her life or through her death. We can believe that God can use her homegoing as a means of fulfilling not only Suzan's purposes, but also His purposes for others.

GOD SEES THE FUTURE

Yet a fourth truth that I have faced regarding God's timing is this: *God sees a future we cannot see.* He is both omnipresent and omniscient, which means that He alone fully sees the ending from the beginning and knows precisely when to act for our full benefit.

Don Hawkins sent me the verse of Scripture: "The good men perish; the godly die before their time and no one seems to care or wonder why. No one seems to realize that God is taking them away from evil days ahead" (Isa. 57:1 TLB).

We have caught glimpses of this truth in our situation with Suzan. Our daughter was facing a lung transplant, an operation that has a high risk of failure. Many people who receive lung transplants—at this current state of transplant technology—live relatively short periods of time. We do not know the pain and suffering that Suzan *might* have been spared.

When we wonder about God's timing, we must remind

ourselves that none of us can look around the corner of the future and see what lies ahead. Only God can see and comprehend all things in the future. When we put our trust in an all-knowing God to act in our best interest at all times, we have hope, and ultimately hope is a vital part of healing for those in grief.

Romans 8:28 (NKJV) declares that "all things work together for good" to those of us who are Christians. It does not say that every single incident is good. While the loss of my precious daughter at an age when she was just reaching the peak of her life may not make any sense to me, with my limited understanding of time and the future, I still can trust that God in His *infinite* understanding of time and eternity has acted out of mercy and love in calling Suzan home to Himself. He has worked all things together for her good, and He is working all things together for our good as well.

Furthermore, I have full assurance that Suzan has boundless joy. As much as we might have held out the marriage of a daughter or the birth of grandchildren as moments of joy that Suzan missed on this earth, I have peace and satisfaction in knowing that every moment that Suzan might have lingered longer on this earth was a moment in which she would have missed out on the ultimate joy that is now hers.

TRUSTING GOD *NOT* TO ANSWER OUR QUESTIONS

I have found that in some cases when we ask *why* of God, He answers us. His answer may give us a complete sense of understanding, or it may give us only a partial insight into His wisdom. In those cases, we must rest in the truth that

God has revealed to us what He has felt is satisfactory for us to know. We must recognize that God calls us always to trust Him and to put our faith in Him. He does not call us to be all-knowing; rather, He calls us to rely upon the fact that *He* is all-knowing and all-loving.

What are we to do when we feel that God does not answer our *why* questions at all or not in a way that we can perceive and understand the answer? Our role as Christians is to trust God completely and, yes, even blindly. His purposes ultimately are beyond our knowing, even if He reveals a great deal to us. We will never know as fully as He knows! His timing is always perfect, and His plan is always unfolding for the righteous according to divine precision.

To continue to dwell on *why* questions and "if only" conjectures is unfruitful and can lead to bitterness and misery, which are burdens a loving God does not want us to carry. We get beyond the *why* questions by trusting that He not only *has* an answer, but that He *is* the Answer. I'm more than content to know that Suzan has all of her *why* questions answered by her Lord.

Pastor Jim Lewis said at Suzan's funeral, "When we get to heaven and we see Jesus in all of His glory, in all of His majesty, in all of His splendor, there will be but two words that we will say concerning the questions of life: 'Of course.' *Of course!* One glimpse of Him will be all that we shall need for the rest of eternity concerning the mysteries of life."

7

NO DOUBT
ABOUT IT!

TWO YEARS BEFORE Suzan's death, I used some of the airline points that I had acquired in my travels to send Suzan to California to spend a week with Cindy and Richard. They had a marvelous time and, in many ways, grew even closer. As I reflected on that memory, the thought came, *If I could send Suzan anywhere I chose, where would I want to send her?*

The answer was immediately obvious. Although I didn't choose to send Suzan home to be with the Lord, there is nowhere I could possibly send her on earth that would approach the beauty, joy, and splendor of the place where she now is.

I have absolutely no doubt about *where* Suzan is or about *what* the nature of her life is there. The answers to the *where* and *what* questions are even more important, in my opinion, and certainly more beneficial to me than answers to the *why* questions. These answers relate to Suzan's present and future, whereas all *why* questions relate only to her past.

Answers to *where* and *what* questions flow from our faith and build our faith, whereas *why* questions tend to keep us in fear and sadness. Answers to *where* and *what* put our focus on the fulfillment of our lives, the success we will know in arriving in heaven, whereas answers to *why* questions keep us wondering about failures or shortcomings on this earth.

"I WONDER WHAT SHE'S DOING?"

Just three weeks after Suzan's death, the Redhead and I were in Washington, D.C., where I was participating in a unique experience with the Washington Symphony Orchestra. A composer had taken some of my writings and had created a musical score to go with them. I went to Washington with excitement that it might be an opportunity to share in a new setting and with a new audience a philosophy I fervently believe is life changing.

I arose early on the morning of the concert and spent nearly an hour in my Bible, concentrating primarily on Psalm 34 and the wonderful assurances it gives us. The psalmist pointed out that even good people are confronted with troubles. The assurance, however, is that God will see us through difficult times, and His promises are ones in which we can trust completely. What encouragement, and what hope!

As I thought about Suzan that morning, I caught myself asking the question, *I wonder what she's doing right now?* Even as I asked the question, its irony hit me. I don't have to wonder what she is doing, where she is, or how she is doing. I know with certainty that she is with her Savior and Lord, that she is doing magnificently well, and that she is praising and worshiping God.

Then I began to play a little game in my mind by questioning where the other members of my immediate family might be.

My thoughts turned first to Cindy, our second-born daughter, whom I affectionately call Sweetnin'. At 8:30 in the morning, knowing her as I do, I thought she might just be returning from a long walk with her golden retriever, Emmitt, whom she loves with a passion. Even though she was still in shock and pain over Suzan's homegoing, she was probably doing well and going about her daily chores. At least I thought that was what *might* be happening in Cindy's life.

Next my thoughts turned to Julie, our youngest daughter, the one I lovingly call Little One. She has such a big heart for everyone, especially those who need a friend, big sister, advocate, or helper. I suspected that at 8:30 in the morning she might be on her way to help somebody. I could visualize several things she *might* be doing.

How was Julie feeling? I was twelve hundred miles away from her at that point, so I had to face the fact that I didn't truly have a clue about how she was feeling or what she was thinking.

Then my thoughts turned to our son, born nearly ten years after Julie. John Thomas, whom we call Tom, was probably in his office at 8:30 in the morning, perhaps talking to a staff member, answering questions, giving direction and a word of hope. How was Tom feeling? I suspected that Tom was feeling better than he dared hope he might feel at that point in his grief—as long as he remained busy and without much time to reflect on the loss of his sister. Given Tom's very tender heart, I suspected that, like me, he might find a quiet spot—perhaps in the men's room or behind the closed door of his office—to weep for a brief time, then he would dry his eyes and get busy. At least I thought that was what *might* be happening with Tom.

My thoughts turned next to the most important person in my life, the Redhead. I knew exactly where she was at that very moment because she was sitting next to me! I knew how she was doing physically because she told me that she had enjoyed a great night's sleep and she was excited about our Washington trip. But where was she emotionally? While the Redhead shares most of her feelings with me, as I do mine with her, I couldn't help wondering if any two people can ever share everything. How was she feeling? I concluded that she was feeling sad. I could tell that by her voice and see it in her eyes and in her face. Did she have fears or doubts as far as Suzan was concerned? Not a onc. But what precisely was she thinking and feeling? My conclusions were only about what *might* be happening inside her.

I also considered what might be happening to my grandchildren. I thought first about Katherine, the beautiful, vivacious fifteen-year-old who loves the Lord and whom I call Keeper. What was she doing at 8:30 in the morning? I suspected she might still be asleep. I knew that she had not been sleeping well following her mother's death, and since school was out, I thought she probably was taking advantage of the opportunity to sleep in. What was she thinking? I couldn't imagine. How was she feeling? Probably sad, perhaps angry, afraid, puzzled. *Perhaps.*

Then there was Little Lover. That's my affectionate name for Elizabeth, Suzan's daughter who is mentally disabled. What an impact she has had on the family! As she has grown and overcome one obstacle after another, we have realized that she is beautiful, healthy, and eager to express love, and that she has accomplished dramatically more than the doctors predicted she would. I believe she was sent to this earth particularly for her daddy. Her impact on Chad's life has been substantial. She owns him, lock, stock, and barrel. Each day when he arrives home from work, she is standing at the door waiting for him. She jumps up into his arms, cuddles, screams, squeals, and showers love on him. What was Little Lover doing at 8:30 in the morning?

She was probably talking with Julie Jackson, the nanny/therapist who has been a true godsend in her life. Julie loves Little Lover with deep faith and compassion that are wonderful to see. She is magnificent in the way she communicates with Elizabeth, enabling her to do many things she enjoys. Julie has been a rich blessing in our lives and is helping me to identify some sides of my daughter Suzan that I did not fully comprehend. Julie refers to Suzan as the best boss she ever had, her best friend, and someone who influenced her life. I suspected that Little Lover, at that particular moment, *might* have been having fun with Julie Jackson.

And what about my firstborn granddaughter who just completed her high school studies? At eighteen, Amanda is a beautiful young woman. She wants everyone else to call her Amey, but she wants her Grandy to call her Sunshine. What was she doing at 8:30 in the morning? She was probably getting ready for graduation. How was she feeling? I believed she was feeling the exhilaration of the upcoming graduation ceremonies, looking forward to all that it means to be a high school graduate, still pondering where she would be going to college in the fall, and wondering what she would be doing during the coming summer. How was she feeling? As she reflected on her aunt Suzan, I felt certain that while she was sad, her faith assured her that Suzan is with the Lord. Precisely what she was thinking and feeling, I did not know.

And Chad? What about him? I suspected that at 8:30 in the morning he was still at home with the girls since he hadn't yet returned to work full-time. How was he feeling? He must be devastated, heartbroken, bewildered a little at the enormity of his loss and the responsibility he faces at giving his daughters a secure, stable, loving environment. I have no doubt in my heart that he is going to do a great job with his girls, but I suspected that *he* might feel some doubts in this area. *Perhaps.*

In 1993, Cindy and Richard moved to Dallas and came to work with me. Richard made an immediate impact on our company. He is a real can-do and do-it-now guy, and as my son and his two brothers-in-law quickly noted, he brought a new energy level to the company. Where was Richard at precisely 8:30 in the morning? I would have guessed that he was doing something busy, and likely important, at work. How was Richard feeling? I suspected that each time he thought about Suzan, he was saddened and shed a tear since he loved her very much, appreciated her sense of humor, her "outrageous" laugh, and the fact that she always had time to listen and talk. But that was only speculation.

Jim Norman came to my mind. What was Jim doing at 8:30 on that morning of June 2, 1995? I believed he might be in his office, talking with a corporate client or staff member about a way to build our business. Jim deals with grief differently from the way most people do, but in some ways similar to the way I handled my grief during the weeks that followed Suzan's death. When Suzan's health took a dramatic turn for the worse at the end of April, Jim spent many hours at the hospital with Julie and the rest of the family. His "therapy"—and the way he handled his grief—was to write a step-by-step diary, part of which I included at the beginning of this book. His account of the medical facts as well as the feelings of the family and his own feelings was a way of release for him. As Suzan breathed her last, Jim voiced, through tears, two of the most beautiful prayers I have ever heard. He was a source of strength and encouragement to all of us.

How was Jim feeling, three weeks after the day Suzan went home to be with the Lord? I suspected that he closed the door to his office from time to time and wept. Jim is a very private person, but his faith is deep and his commitment is firm. However, I could not be certain about precisely what he was thinking and feeling at that moment.

I also thought about Chachis, the newest member of our family, who is Tom's wife. She is from Campechi, Mexico, and when she arrived in the United States to attend college, she spoke no English, yet she finished her first year in college with a 3.0 grade point average, which to me is an awesome accomplishment. She and Tom met while they were in college. I affectionately call her *Bonita,* which is Spanish for "pretty woman." Where was Bonita at that moment? I felt certain she was at home, perhaps feeding their precious daughter, Alexandra Nicole, whom I have nicknamed Promise because from the first moment I saw her, I knew she had a lot of promise for the future. (Tom has noted that soon Keeper will be baby-sitting her young cousin, Promise, so she truly will be a Promise Keeper!) Perhaps Chachis was playing quietly with Promise.

How was Chachis feeling? I suspected she was feeling a great sense of loss because of all the family members, Suzan had spent the most time with her and probably understood her better than anyone else in the family. I knew Chachis loved Suzan and was saddened by her death. In her quiet moments, she, too, sheds tears of grief. Exactly what she *might* be thinking, feeling, or doing that morning, however, was uncertain to me.

Through these brief reflections on each member of our family, I recognized with joy that I knew a lot about each one. I had a strong awareness of their daily lives and their innermost feelings and faith. I knew that I loved them deeply and respected them highly, and that I would spend eternity with them. In many ways, that is all that is necessary to know about any person. I also recognized that I cherish the moments I have spent with each of them.

And yet I concluded that while I halfway thought I knew what the other members of my family might be doing at 8:30 in the morning on June 2, 1995, I couldn't truly be certain of their whereabouts, their state of mind and heart, or their activities. With Suzan there was a certainty. I found it fascinating that I could be far more confident about where the daughter whom I cannot see—in a physical, human way—was, and how she was doing, than I could be about the family members whom I could reach out and touch, hug, or call on the phone.

I reflected on the fact that while it is wonderful to have a loving, close-knit family who are there in all of the peak and valley times of life, it is even more wonderful to have a heavenly Father who loves us, understands us, and is present with us *always*. The apostle Paul eloquently wrote, "I am persuaded that neither death nor life, nor angels nor principalities nor powers, nor things present nor things to come, nor height nor depth, nor any other created thing, shall be able to separate us from the love of God which is in Christ Jesus our Lord" (Rom. 8:38–39 NKJV).

The Lord's promises are eternal. We rest on the unbreakable promises. I rest in the knowledge that Suzan is forever with God, and though I cannot physically see her this very moment, I will one day see her for an eternity.

Until then, I can imagine all that Suzan might be experiencing, feeling, and thinking. In thinking about my family members on this earth, I always must face the reality that all things might not be perfect, positive, or joyful for them in any given moment. Hardships, pain, and sorrow are parts of earthly life. But with Suzan, I can be certain that *everything* she is experiencing is perfection and joy and exhilaration and filled with the very best of *life*!

Envisioning Suzan in her life in heaven is comforting, and it creates a connection to her. It keeps alive and fresh my relationship with my daughter. Am I imagining things falsely? Perhaps no more so than in my effort to imagine what life was like for each of my family members at one precise moment on this earth. There are things we know about the personality, faith, and character of the person we have lost. Those things have not changed—they have only come to the point of perfection. To think about the one you love in the perfection of all that he was created by God to be, to express, and to do—what a joy that is!

ABSENT, BUT NOT MISSING

There are times, which almost seem to come instantaneously, when our gratitude for Suzan's life is replaced with a sobering thought that she is no longer with us, that our family is no longer complete, and that we will never again be complete as a family on this earth. When we have our family get-togethers, one person is missing. When we celebrate her birthday, she is not present. At Christmas, Easter, Thanksgiving, and all other holiday celebrations we have as a family, her presence is profound because she is not present.

And then the thought comes: *Suzan is not missing; she is merely absent.*

To be absent means not to be present in a particular moment or setting. To be missing means that nobody knows where you are. We know where Suzan is! She is not missing, only absent from us temporarily. The greater truth—and certainly the more wonderful and comforting truth—is that we *will* be with her one day and all of us will worship our Lord eternally together in heaven.

This separation is only temporary. It is only an absence. Our future speaks of togetherness, love, and unspeakable joy.

8

HEAVEN'S
GLORY

WHEN PEOPLE ASKED me, "How are you doing?" in the aftermath of Suzan's death, I often replied, "Better than good!" I could say that only because of my faith that Suzan is also doing better than good, and she is residing in a place that is better than wonderful.

For many years I held to the belief, *I've got so many things to do and so many people I love, I hope God will let me live to a ripe old age so I can get these things done and be with the people I love so much.* Since Suzan's death, I have come to a new realization: *At whatever time God calls me home, His timing will be perfect, and the place that He has prepared for me will be perfect.* I have more to look forward to in heaven than I have to look forward to by experiencing a long life on this earth.

The words to the gospel song often come to mind:

> When we all get to heaven,
> What a day of rejoicing that will be!

> When we all see Jesus,
> We'll sing and shout the victory!

How true those words ring out in my heart. Now, please don't read a death wish into my statement. I am ready, but not anxious, to die. God has given me wonderful peace of mind on earth while reminding me of the many benefits that will be mine once I am in heaven with Him.

Earth is a "sometimes joy" experience. As deeply as we might know Christ, and as much as we might have faith in Him, our joy here is not constant because we live in a world of circumstances that frequently rob us of joy. Heaven, on the other hand, is an "always joy" experience. It is a place of supreme happiness. I am content to be here in today's happiness, but I am eager at the same time to arrive there and experience eternity's joy.

GLORIOUSLY AND FULLY ALIVE

An encouraging aspect of my Christian faith and my trust in Jesus Christ is the fact that during His ministry here on earth, Christ never attended a funeral at which He did not raise the dead. Jesus *is* the Resurrection. He plainly said of Himself, "I am the resurrection and the life. He who believes in Me, though he may die, he shall live. And whoever lives and believes in Me shall never die" (John 11:25–26 NKJV).

The resurrection of Jesus is a vital matter to you and me. Dr. Ike Reighard has pointed out that one of the most beautiful things about the resurrection of Jesus is this: the huge stone at the tomb "couldn't keep Jesus in the grave, and the walls in the Upper Room couldn't keep Jesus out of that room." As Christians, we are going to be able to move to and fro when we get to heaven because we will be gloriously alive! We are going to be more alive and feel more alive than we have ever been or felt in this current existence.

There have been times in my life when I have felt vibrantly and enthusiastically and fully alive—as if every cell in my body were energized. Those moments, however, come and go. Nobody can sustain that degree of vitality for long periods of time. Once we are with the Lord, however, that satisfying and exhilarating feeling of life—and even more so—will be the norm.

At Suzan's funeral, Pastor Jim Lewis said, "The past few days you heard that Suzan Witmeyer is dead. Don't you believe it! She is more alive than she has ever been." Oh, how true that is!

A PERSONAL WELCOME
BY OUR LORD JESUS

The Scriptures tell us that when the first Christian martyr, Stephen, was about to enter heaven, he saw Jesus Christ, who was seated at the right hand of God, literally stand up to welcome him home to Himself. (See Acts 7:55–56.) I believe Jesus stands up to welcome every believer who has made the same commitment Stephen made. We are welcomed into eternity by the One who made eternity possible for us. The psalmist proclaimed, "When I awake in heaven, I will be fully satisfied, for I will see you face to face" (Ps. 17:15 TLB).

I have every reason to know that the Lord was present and stood up the moment Suzan entered His presence, because Jesus said to those who loved and followed Him, "Lo, I am with you always" (Matt. 28:20 NKJV). In addition

He said, "Where two or three have gathered together in My name, there I am in their midst" (Matt. 18:20 NASB). It goes far beyond that, as we learn from the psalmist:

> *O LORD, You have searched me and known me.*
> *You know my sitting down and my rising up;*
> *You understand my thought afar off.*
> *You comprehend my path and my lying down,*
> *And are acquainted with all my ways.*
> *For there is not a word on my tongue,*
> *But behold, O LORD, You know it altogether. (Ps. 139:1–4 NKJV)*

Yes, our Lord was at the party that welcomed Suzan into His presence.

SURROUNDED BY LOVED ONES

My pastor of twenty years, Dr. W. A. Criswell, once was asked, "Will we know our loved ones when we get to heaven?" He responded as only he could: "We won't know our loved ones—really know them—*until* we get to heaven."

I have often told people that I know precisely what I want to do when I get to heaven. First, I want to see and worship my Lord. Next, I want to see Suzan. Then, I want to visit with my mother and father, my brothers and sisters and friends. I know it is going to be a magnificent reunion. Even so, I don't believe the mind of man is capable of imagining what those heavenly reunions are *really* going to be like.

It is very easy for me to imagine that Suzan is spending a great deal of time in heaven with my mother, whom Suzan always felt was one of the wisest, most godly women she ever knew. Suzan never met either of her grandfathers, but she knew and deeply loved her maternal grandmother who always had plenty of Coca-Cola and even asparagus especially for her. Suzan's giggle, warm hugs, and sense of humor definitely came by way of her maternal grandmother. Now she spends time with all of those family members.

A GLORIFIED BODY—HEALTHY
AND VIVACIOUS

When I see Suzan in heaven with my eyes of faith, I never see her moving slowly, as she did her last few months on earth. I see her moving smoothly and quickly and easily, just as she did in her younger years. I know with certainty that she has been restored to even better health than she experienced on earth.

Suzan has no trouble breathing. She is not coughing. She is able to sing and laugh as loud as she desires. She has a new and glorious body, one of total health and vitality. Paul informed us,

> *There are also celestial bodies and terrestrial bodies; but the glory of the celestial is one, and the glory of the terrestrial is another. There is one glory of the sun, another glory of the moon, and another glory of the stars; for one star differs from another star in glory. So also is the resurrection of the dead. The body is sown in corruption, it is raised in incorruption. It is sown in dishonor, it is raised in glory. It is sown in weakness, it is raised in power.* (1 Cor. 15:40–43 NKJV)

With his unique sense of humor, Dr. Reighard has pointed out that this means we will never again have to be probed and poked or made to suffer all of the other indignities that people often experience when they are sick or dying. The very day I was reflecting upon his words, I went to see a physician, and yes, I experienced some poking and probing! I was glad the physician was there and able to solve my small problem, but I am even more grateful that when I stand in front of the Lord, I will have a perfect body and no probing or poking will ever again be necessary.

Our bodies now may disappoint us, but when they are raised, they will be beautiful and glorious in every way. Our bodies now may be weak or sickly, but in heaven, they will be full of power, strength, and energy.

What a comfort it is for me to know that Suzan now has unlimited energy, perfect health, and perfect peace. When people ask me about my family, I often say—and with all honesty—that one of my children is in perfect health and the other three are in good health. I know that is true!

Our resurrection bodies will be incorruptible. Most of us would like to make a few changes in the bodies we have here on earth. There are always a few ways in which we wish we were a little more healthy, a little more fit, a little more youthful. But when we get to heaven, we won't in our wildest imaginations desire any changes in our bodies because they will be perfect. They will work precisely as God created them to work—*forever*!

A REAL BODY—JUST LIKE THE ONE JESUS HAS

In Philippians 3:20–21 (NLT) we read, "We are citizens of heaven, where the Lord Jesus Christ lives. And we are eagerly waiting for him to return as our Savior. He will take these weak mortal bodies of ours and change them into glorious bodies like his own, using the same mighty power that he will use to conquer everything, everywhere." We are going to have the same kind of body that Jesus Christ had after His resurrection. But what kind of body is that?

Jesus appeared to His disciples and said, "Look at my hands! Look at my feet! You can see that it is I, myself! Touch me and make sure that I am not a ghost! For ghosts don't have bodies, as you see that I do!" (Luke 24:39 TLB). As Jesus spoke, He no doubt held out His hands for them to see. He showed them the wound in His side and His nail-pierced feet. The disciples were simultaneously filled with joy, wonder, and *doubt.* Then He asked them, "Do you have anything here to eat?" (Luke 24:41 TLB). They gave Him a piece of broiled fish, and He ate it while they watched.

Dr. Reighard elaborated on this point in a sermon, and he noted that in our glorified bodies, "We're not going to be up there just floating around. We're going to have identity, and it's going to be permanent. We're going to have a personality. We're not going to be ghosts." Knowing this is encouraging to me. We are going to have bodies, and people will recognize us for who we are.

Jesus by His very example and by His Word taught us that we are going to have bodies that can be touched. They will be capable of being seen as well as hugged and held. They will have substance. I find comfort in knowing that I will recognize Suzan in heaven and that I will be able to touch her, hug her, and kiss her—as well as the other relatives and friends awaiting me.

Paul spoke to this issue: "For we know that when this tent we live in now is taken down—when we die and leave these bodies—we will have wonderful new bodies in heaven, homes that will be ours forevermore, made for us by God himself, and not by human hands" (2 Cor. 5:1 TLB). Paul was telling us that the difference between our natural bodies and the glorified bodies is like the difference between living in a flimsy tent and living in a permanent house. The glorified body is not subject to the same limitations that we experience in the earthly body. It is a lasting body, immortal, and one that will never wear out.

We can also conclude from Jesus' example of eating fish by the Sea of Galilee with His disciples that we are going to be eating in our new heavenly bodies. Again, I don't believe our imaginations can conceive of the banquet table our Lord is going to set for us. I believe it's going to be absolutely magnificent, with delicious dishes never before tasted on this earth.

Recently I told the Redhead that when I get to heaven, I am going to be able to eat all of the Baskin-Robbins lemon custard ice cream I want and not gain an ounce. The Redhead smiled and said, "Honey, I'll bet there's going to be something even better than that!" She's right, of course. Our "land of milk and honey" on this earth, where we talk so much about calories and cholesterol, is nothing like heaven, where we will be able to experience the best of everything without any negative side effects whatsoever. The Lord will provide for us the things that are not only for our benefit, but that also will delight us completely—and He alone knows precisely what these things are.

THE "REAL US" WILL BE FULLY BIRTHED

Benjamin Franklin wrote to Elizabeth Hubbard on February 2, 1756, saying, "I send my condolences to you, and we have lost a dear and a valuable relation. But it's the will of God and it's the nature that these mortal bodies be laid aside when the soul is to enter into real life, because it's rather an embryo state that we're in."

Benjamin Franklin, one of the greatest thinkers this country ever produced, looked at the human life as we experience it and said we're in an embryonic state, just as if we are in a mother's womb. He considered this life to be merely a preparation for *real* living. That is something I had never considered before, but it is certainly something I believe also.

Benjamin Franklin went on to write,

A man is not completely born until he is dead. Why then should we grieve that a new child has been born above with the immortals, that a new member has been added to their happy families? That bodies should be lent to us is a kind and a benevolent act of God. When they become unfit for the purposes that are afforded us, and it becomes pain with our bodies rather than pleasure, and instead of an aid these bodies have become an encumbrance and they answer none of the intentions for which they were given, it is equally kind and benevolent that God has provided a way that we can get rid of these bodies. And death is that way. We ourselves often prudently choose a partial death. In some cases it may be a mangled limb which cannot be restored and it's amputated. It may be he who plucks out a tooth, and parts with it freely, since the pain goes with it. And thus a person surrenders the whole body and departs at once and with it goes all of the pain and all of the possibilities of pain, all disease and all suffering. Thus we're invited to go abroad on a party of pleasure that's to last forever. Perhaps a loved one has gone on before us. We could not all conveniently start together. And why should we be grieved at this, because we're going to be soon to follow. And we know where to find him or where to find her that knows Christ.

The real you is not your body. The real you is a spirit housed in a body. The spirit lives on, and it is clothed with a body that is ideally suited for heaven, not earth. What a glorious body we will have for the glorious place we will call our eternal home!

AN EVERLASTING HOME OF JOY AND BEAUTY

My friend Tony Zeiss described for me the experience he and his wife, Beth, enjoyed on the island of Oahu as he played the mountain golf courses there. He went into elaborate detail describing the breathtaking beauty. I have every reason to believe that heaven is even more beautiful. In fact, the very best island paradise I can imagine doesn't hold a candle to the beauty that Suzan is beholding. Furthermore, Tony and Beth could spend only a few days on Oahu. Suzan is enjoying the most exquisite beauty of all creation *forever.*

On January 14, 1998, our pastor, Dr. Jack Graham, preached on heaven. He chose Revelation 22:1–5 (NKJV) as his text:

> *And he [the angel] showed me a pure river of water of life, clear as crystal, proceeding from the throne of God and of the Lamb. In the middle of its street, and on either side of the river, was the tree of life, which bore twelve fruits, each tree yielding its fruit*

every month. The leaves of the tree were for the healing of the nations. And there shall be no more curse, but the throne of God and of the Lamb shall be in it, and His servants shall serve Him. They shall see His face, and His name shall be on their foreheads. There shall be no night there: They need no lamp nor light of the sun, for the Lord God gives them light. And they shall reign forever and ever.

I found Dr. Graham's sermon very encouraging, and I want to share some of what he said with you:

Heaven is the bright spot for us, the hope for our hearts in an otherwise ever-increasingly darkening world. The promise of a place where there is no more night, no more despair, no more darkness, no more doubt, no more fear, no more failure, no more sin, no more suffering, no more heartache must encourage the heart of the believer to no end, because now we have a mission.

Heaven is not only a destination; it is a motivation. Heaven is a present reality to the believer, and the longer we live, the more we experience life, the more homesick for heaven we become. Heaven is not a fantasy; it is a fact.

The fact, however, that we cannot describe heaven with human language demonstrates its reality! There are things real, there are things perfect, that we could never describe, but here is what we know. Heaven is not a state of mind. Heaven is not swimming around in eternity through some kind of supernatural cyberspace. Heaven is not wispy. It is not ethereal. It is not vaporous. Heaven is a real place that exists in a time and in a dimension beyond this world and beyond this life. Yes, heaven is a literal place.

The Bible describes heaven as "up." The Bible

describes heaven as "beyond the heavens," which are the atmospheric heavens as we know them. With our puny ability to search the galaxies and also the material world in which we live, we don't know where heaven is located. Nevertheless, there is a heaven. There is a Royal City. There is a New Jerusalem.

But in another sense, heaven exists in a time and in a dimension that is all around us *right now*. Heaven and this life are connected. You say, "How do you know that, Pastor?" In Old Testament times when Elisha and his servant were facing impending death and disaster, and the servant was shaking in his sandals and was afraid for his life, Elisha began to pray, "Oh, God, open his eyes that he may see!" And God opened the eyes of that servant and he saw all around him the heavenly host of God—angels charged with the assignment of protecting Elisha and his servant. (See 2 Kings 6:16–17.) Heaven was all around them. It was invisible to all but Elisha, and then his servant, in that moment. Nevertheless, it was present in its unseen reality. It was in another dimension.

All around us at all times are the saints of all ages. Around us are those who are in the life that is to come. Around us are family and friends, loved ones, saints of God who form a great "cloud of witnesses" (Heb. 12:1 NKJV). Heaven is not simply "out there somewhere" far, far away, but it is closer than we know. It is *now*. Heaven is all around us. It requires eyes of faith to see it. Paul wrote to the Corinthians, "Now we see through a mirror darkly." (See 1 Cor. 13:12.) How true that is! Nevertheless, our inability to see does not diminish the reality that the presence of God, the presence of the angelic host, the presence of the saints of the ages, the presence and power of God's kingdom is all around us. Heaven is real.

John tells us that this heaven is real and substantive—not merely vaporous clouds filled with people floating about like ghosts. He tells us in the book of Revelation that heaven is a city, a country, and that it has streets and gates and houses and thrones and drivers and people. If anything, heaven is *too real* for language. It is the ultimate land of the living.

I remember when I heard Dr. Howard Hendricks say years ago, "We think that we're living in the land of the living on our way to the land of the dying, when in fact we are in the land of the dying on our way to the land of the living!" We live in a dying world. We live in a disintegrating and temporal world—on our way to a permanent and eternal world.

What does John tell us about heaven? He tells us about a river that runs through it. That river is pure, clear as crystal, and it flows from the throne of God and from the Lamb. In the middle of the street and on either side of the river, the tree of life is to be found. In Revelation 21:6 (NKJV) he says, "I will give of the fountain of the water of life freely to him who thirsts." This water will be a streaming, glorious, glistening, gushing flow of life, so powerful that we will drink and never thirst.

Psalm 46:4 (NKJV) tells us, "There is a river whose streams shall make glad the city of God." This resplendent river reflects the awesome presence of God and the glory of God, who sits upon the throne. This river represents the inexhaustible supply flowing from God's presence—His love and His grace will satisfy our thirst forever.

Contrast this to hell. In a parable of Jesus, the rich man who was in hell prayed that someone would come and just take a drop of water and touch it to his tongue.

His thirst was great and unquenchable. But in the eternal abode of believers there is an inexhaustible supply of grace and mercy. There is no end to the blessing, no end to the provision, no end to life. We will drink forever out of the wells of salvation.

On either side of this river grows the tree of life. Most Bible scholars believe the language here refers to a great and beautiful forest of the trees of life. These trees yield fruit—not only "in season," but in every season. Nothing ever dies in heaven—it just keeps growing and keeps producing. When the fruit is eaten, it produces healing of the nations. The word for *healing* here is the same root word for *therapeutic.* Heavenly health food is available! Heaven will have no disease, and the healing of the nations will be pervasive. This refers to a renewed vitality and renewed strength—not simply the absence of disease, but a genuine well-being and wholeness. There will be no disease, but even beyond that state of wellness, there will be vitality and satisfaction and inner well-being and peace.

Together, the river of life and the trees of life produce a *fullness* of life.

Are we going to eat in heaven? Yes, absolutely. I'm looking forward to it. John describes the marriage supper of the Lamb. And I just know they're going to serve chicken fried steak, mashed potatoes and gravy, and my cholesterol count won't go up a bit. To that my associate minister of music, Todd Bell, says, "Hallelujah!"

We will experience in heaven "no more curse" (Rev. 22:3 NKJV). The curses that were put on man, woman, and creation in Genesis 3:16–19 will be removed. The earth today bears the ugly scars and the dirty stains of sin, but in the new creation, the curse is cursed! There will be no

more violence, no more upheaval, no more pain or difficulty or hardship. We will live in perfect security. You
won't even have to lock your doors in heaven because
there will be no more effect of sin. There will be no more
contending with Satan, dealing with evil, or struggling
with temptation. There will be no more pain, no more
sorrow, no more suffering, no more death, no funeral
processions moving up the streets of glory, no graves on
the hillsides, no funeral dirges in the presence of the
Lamb who is the Resurrection and the Life. There will be
no more curse—only peace and pleasure and security
and satisfaction. None of us has ever lived in a world like
that, but we will. *We will!* We will know one day what it
means to live without any curse.

John tells us that the reason there is no more curse is
because the throne of God and the Lamb "shall be in it."
Heaven will be governed by God. God and the Lamb are
one and the same. When you get to heaven, you will not
see three gods—God the Father over here, God the Son
over there, and God the Holy Spirit in still another place.
We do not worship three gods. There is one God—God
and Father of our Lord Jesus Christ is the same God who
sits upon the throne is the same dear Lamb is the same
God who reconciled us unto Himself. And when you look
into the face of God in the pure light of eternity, you will
see the face of Jesus Christ. For at His feet every knee
shall bow and every tongue shall confess that He is Lord
to the glory of God. Jesus Christ is Lord. He rules His
kingdom. He is unrivaled.

In our time on this earth, it may appear to us on
occasion that God is getting the short end of a long stick.
It often appears to us that everything is getting worse and
worse, that God is being more and more removed from

our society and removed from our minds. But in that day, His time, the one and only King of kings, Lord of lords, the only potentate Jesus Christ shall reign forever and ever. We shall see Him, and He shall rule His kingdom with an everlasting reign. His servants shall continue to serve Him, on and on and on and on. We in heaven will serve the Lord continuously. As individuals, we will serve Him with a pure heart and a pure motivation. We will serve Him with incredible accomplishments, doing great things for God, engaging in tasks that we cannot even begin to imagine. God may very well assign us to other solar systems and galaxies to proclaim the glory of excellence! We will serve Him day and night, for all eternity!

In heaven, we will have no failure, no frustration. Imagine serving someone that you love perfectly, doing something that you enjoy preeminently, and doing it in a body that is forever energized. In heaven we will never grow tired in our ceaseless activity of service.

In Revelation 22:4 (NKJV) John writes that we shall "see His face, and His name shall be on [our] foreheads." What does it mean to be marked by Jesus in this way? It means that we will have His character, His righteousness, His nature. We will be identified as His. We will reflect His glory.

Furthermore, we shall see Him face-to-face. The ultimate bliss, the ultimate blessedness, the ultimate beauty of heaven is the profound joy of seeing Jesus face-to-face. None of us has ever seen this in our lifetime. We walk by faith. Peter spoke of those who would serve Jesus even though they hadn't seen Him—we are the ones he was writing about.

We must be careful that we never miss the central point of heaven. What is that point? It is that we will be face-to-face with Jesus Christ. Heaven isn't heaven without Jesus. He is the centerpiece, the ultimate, the star attraction. And we will reign with Him, be reunited with Him, and be rewarded by Him. We will serve Him, world without end, in His eternal kingdom where there is no more night, no more sin, and no more suffering. All of heaven is Jesus centered, and so must our lives be now.

HEAVEN IS SIMPLY BETTER

Only one thing could be better than a joyful life in Christ here on this earth, and that is a life of joy with Christ in heaven. It is the glory of heaven, and being aware of all that a departed loved one now experiences, that truly takes the pain out of death. As much as we think we may have learned how to live, and even to live an abundant life, we won't truly know what it means to live until we have died!

Life in heaven will be so much more invigorating, fulfilling, and glorious than anything we have experienced. Even our best day of vitality and health will not come close to the perfection we will feel in our bodies in heaven. As Dwight L. Moody lay on his deathbed, his dying words were these: "Do not keep me from my coronation today. Why, this is death? It's better than living!"

And so it is now for your departed loved one, and so it will be for you one day!

9

APPRECIATING ALL OF GOD'S MIRACLE MOMENTS

ON JUNE 9, 1995, Captain Scott O'Grady was rescued several days after his jet had been shot down over Bosnia. In the press conference and interviews that followed his rescue, he consistently credited the role God had played in his rescue, and he spoke about his faith in God. I was surprised, therefore, when not one word related to his faith or God was included in the newscast that I heard on one of the morning programs the next day. It seemed obvious to me that the media were not going to recognize God's hand in his rescue, or that the media had chosen to overlook the role that faith had played in Captain O'Grady's life.

To me, everything about the fact that Captain O'Grady was still alive and had been rescued without injury or further loss of American life was miraculous. Surely when one looks at this situation from the point of human logic, Scott O'Grady should not have even been alive to be rescued. His parachute kept him aloft for several minutes above hostile territory, in clear view of a nearby town and in close proximity to a truck filled with Bosnian soldiers. He had only a couple of minutes to disengage himself from his parachute and run toward nearby shrubbery after he landed in a small clearing. Even so, he was not found. At times, soldiers came within six feet of the places where he hid himself, and yet something clouded the curiosity and eyesight of the searchers to prevent them from finding him.

Captain O'Grady survived for six long days by hiding during the daytime hours and moving from one location to another between midnight and four o'clock in the morning. Lack of food was a problem to him, but lack of water was a bigger problem. One night as he prayed that God might let it rain, God sent him a deluge.

All of these things are miraculous! How much more meaningful any life experience is, and what joy and comfort it gives to the human heart, when we *choose to see the miraculous* in all things. Every minute of life, every experience, has a touch of the miraculous in it. We are wise to look for it, acknowledge it, and rejoice in it because the miraculous is evident even in losing a loved one.

NO COINCIDENCES IN GOD'S PLAN

God is sovereign, and there are no coincidences in His plans and purposes. *Coincidence* is a man-made word. Miracles are God-made realities.

After I committed my life to Christ, an incredible series of circumstances unfolded that some people would no doubt describe as coincidences. Someone said that coincidence is only God's way of remaining anonymous. I don't make a big issue of these things, but I do try to recognize God's hand at work in even very subtle ways. His miracles—

both large and small—are around us continuously, and we need to recognize and appreciate them.

It is easy to see God's hand at work in Steve Brown's story of "One Red Rose" in his January 1998 *KeyLife* publication. It is paraphrased and summarized here.

A mother was terminally ill, and her daughter had occasion to spend a great deal of time talking with her in her final days. In one of their conversations the daughter said to the mother, "Mom, could we have a secret, something just between us? I know it's going to sound crazy, but if you die, when you get to heaven, if it's more than you ever dreamed it would be, if you are all right and see God and Jesus, would you send me one red rose?" It was a special moment between them, one the daughter described as "almost an eternal moment."

The mother responded, "Yes, I'll do that."

A week later the daughter said, "Look, Mom, about our secret. I'll be on earth and you'll be heaven. How are you going to get a rose to me?" The mother replied, "God can do anything!"

Shortly after these conversations, the mother died. With everything she had to do, the daughter forgot about the secret she and her mother shared. Then, in her own words, here's what happened: "All of a sudden in the back of the funeral home I caught a glimpse of an elderly gentleman with a cane. I didn't know him. I was sure I had never seen him before. I turned and looked at him. As he knelt down at my mother's coffin, he placed into her hands *just one beautiful red rose*. I walked over and asked the gentleman what had made him bring the rose. He said, 'Oh, honey, it's been on my mind all day. All day I've been thinking about it. I just knew I had to get one red rose for your mother.'"

Steve Brown at this point in telling the story quickly

assured his readers that he was not into the New Age and that he didn't believe in having séances or in communicating with the dead. But he also pointed out that sometimes God, in His infinite graciousness and love, will for just a moment pull back the curtain and allow us to see beyond our limited view of life and death. Steve believes what happened in that woman's life was one of those occasions.

Although I cannot say anything like that happened to our family in the aftermath of Suzan's death, I do believe it is more than a mere coincidence that we experienced a miracle in our yard.

Gardenias were Suzan's favorite flower, and we have three gardenia bushes in our yard. Those who knew Suzan knew of her love for gardenias. One of the most tender expressions of love that we witnessed after Suzan died was the gift of gardenias provided by her in-laws, Don and Babe Witmeyer.

The Witmeyers asked if they could provide the flowers to place on top of Suzan's casket. Every florist they contacted, however, responded the same way to their request for a casket covering of gardenias: "Sorry, we are sold out." Mother's Day gift orders had completely depleted their supplies of the one flower that the Witmeyers sought to buy. That slowed the Witmeyers in their quest, but it did not stop them. They bought every gardenia bush from nurseries for miles around, even if the bush had only one bloom, until they had enough blossoms to cover Suzan's entire casket. The bushes were later planted in Suzan and Chad's yard.

In the years since Suzan's death, none of us in the family can see or smell a gardenia without thinking of Suzan. Several times various ones of us have picked gardenias from our yards and put them on Suzan's grave.

So what was the miracle we experienced?

Several weeks after Suzan died, the Redhead and I returned home from a somewhat disappointing business trip, and as we pulled into our driveway, the Redhead excitedly said, "Look, we planted that bush more than eight years ago, and it has a gardenia on it for the very first time!"

Seeing this bush in bloom was almost like receiving a "welcome home" message from Suzan herself. Then we realized that all of our flower beds were ablaze with color. Julie and Cindy had been there to plant flowers. We couldn't help crying, to a great extent because of our daughters' generosity, but also because there was a story associated with this act of love.

Our children had planned to surprise their mother with beds full of flowers for Mother's Day. Because of Suzan's shortage of energy, Cindy and Julie had planned to enlist only Suzan's supervisory skills and also let her procure the soft drinks and ice water to keep them refreshed. All of the children had pooled their money to buy the flowers, and the girls were planning to do the planting on Saturday, April 29, when they knew their mother was scheduled to be out of town. Suzan was rushed to the hospital the night before, and as it turned out, she died the day before Mother's Day. The planting of the flowers had obviously been postponed until the girls felt they could face the project without Suzan. Their belated Mother's Day gift greeted us upon our return home.

The following year we got another miracle. The gardenia bushes bloomed long before gardenias are supposed to bloom in our region of the country. And one of the bushes was full of more blooms than we had ever seen on a gardenia bush.

We believe these blooming gardenia bushes were one of God's ways of communicating to us the glorified life that

Suzan now enjoys. A brilliant display of blossoms on our gardenia bushes was a sign to us of the beauty that now surrounds Suzan continually and eternally.

GIFTS THAT SPEAK OF GOD'S GREAT LOVE

I experienced numerous other miracle moments after Suzan's death. Each of them spoke to me in a special way of God's tender provision and care. I want to share a few of them with you.

The day after Suzan's funeral, I went to the dentist. I was exhausted physically and emotionally, and I literally fell asleep three times in the dentist's chair. When I left the dental office, I drove a few blocks, and as I signaled to turn left, I was startled to look into my rearview mirror and see the flashing lights of a police car behind me. I was puzzled about what I could have done that warranted being stopped by the police.

As Officer George Sparks approached my car, I pulled out my driver's license and handed it to him when he got to my car window. He very pleasantly asked me if I realized I was going thirty-three miles an hour in a school zone. I told him no, I had not realized I was in a school zone. I quickly added that I was not denying I was speeding in a school zone, but that I had not seen the school zone sign. Looking at my driver's license, he asked me if I was *the* Zig Ziglar. I assured him I was. Then he said, "Didn't you just lose a loved one?"

At that point, I lost it. When I broke down and began weeping he told me that he was not only a fan of my work, but more important, also a brother in the Lord. I explained to him that my oldest daughter had just died, and he was very compassionate. The young man truly ministered to me that day, even in the very unlikely situation of being pulled over for a traffic violation. Was it a coincidence that God had put him there to awaken me to the fact that I was not driving alertly? Was it a coincidence that the one who stopped me that day was a brother in the Lord who encouraged me? Perhaps, but I much prefer to believe that a loving heavenly Father, in a thousand and one different ways, is still looking after a son in a special way.

GOD'S GIFT OF PERFECT TIMING

One week after Suzan's death, I found myself headed back home after a two-and-a-half-day speaking engagement with EIG (Exit Information Guide) in Orlando, Florida. It seemed impossible to believe that Suzan had been gone only a week—it seemed like forever. I was also astonished at the amount of healing that God had already worked in my life. In many ways, it had been the toughest week of my life, and yet I had peace and assurance deep within that God was with me and Suzan was with Him.

The event in Orlando had been scheduled for some time. It was a small group, and I had asked the Lord before I went to give me the courage and right opportunities to witness effectively for Him. At the conclusion of my presentation, I told the people about how much I loved Suzan, how much we in her family missed her, and yet how confident we were that she was safely in the loving arms of Christ. There wasn't a dry eye in the room, including my own, and I felt that God had blessed my message to them in a supernatural way.

Prior to that time, God had used my witness in my career in marvelous ways, and I had been quick to share biblical principles and examples with others. I had always made it clear that I am a Christian and that I believe Jesus Christ to be the answer to every person's life.

Never before, however, had I witnessed so boldly to a group of people in a business setting. I feel that it could have been the only group that would have received my message in such a responsive, loving, and caring way. It is a small company with good, sincere, honest, hardworking people who truly represent Middle America. Their beliefs seemed to make my sharing more acceptable. In any case, I am firmly convinced that the circumstances surrounding the engagement contributed to the openness and boldness I felt—the length of time I had spent individually with the leaders in the company, the ride we took from Gainesville to Orlando, the hour-and-a-half session of questions and answers, the dinner we had with the owner's family. All of those factors combined to enable me to feel rapport with the group.

Was it a coincidence that I spoke to just that group at just that time? I don't believe so. And that was made more evident when I later learned that the president of the company, who had held the belief that you should not mix "religion with business," was very moved by my presentation. He was impressed that his people were so moved as I shared the loss of my daughter with them. Since the meeting, "closet Christians" have come out all over the company, and he has been talking with them about Christ. God is amazing, and He really can and does take any situation and use it for His glory.

GOD'S REMINDERS UNDERSCORE HIS PURPOSES

There are times, I believe, when God's miracle moments come to us to underscore His presence with us and to assure us in rather profound ways that His purposes *are* being accomplished. One such instance happened to me on March 6, 1996. I was in Phoenix, Arizona, to speak, and I had dinner with Mike Ingram and sixteen other outstanding Christians. The men and women had come together to devote an entire evening to discussing how they served the Lord and helped their fellowman.

As the host of the dinner, Mike went around the table, asking each person to comment about who he was and what he did. When the time came for me to share my faith, I decided to share how Suzan had first come to know the Lord. As I started to speak about her commitment to Christ, an incredible thing happened. The "Hallelujah Chorus" came on over the piped-in sound system. At first I didn't realize what was happening, but as I shared more about Suzan's faith, the circumstances leading up to her death, the impact of her death on my life, and the blessed assurance that I had felt in knowing she is safe with the Lord, the "Hallelujah Chorus" got louder and louder.

The men and women were awestruck, as I was, and one man who was a member of the club where we were dining commented that in his thirty-five years of membership, he had never once heard any kind of spiritual or religious music played over the sound system. Cynics and skeptics might say that was a coincidence, but knowing and loving my Lord as I do, I believe that was a divine moment, a way for God to express His reassurance to me that Suzan is with the Lord and the angels in heaven really are singing with joy at her presence.

MIRACLE MOMENTS ARE AMONG
GOD'S "JOY GIFTS"

At times, I believe, God gives us miraculous moments so that we will have a burst of joy in an otherwise sad season of our lives. I don't know any person who is sad in the out-working of a miracle, even a miracle that may be considered small in the eyes of the world.

Nine days after Suzan died, I was scheduled to play in the annual golf and tennis day sponsored by Prestonwood Baptist Church in Dallas. My sons-in-law, my son, my wife, and I are all golf enthusiasts. (Yours truly is no doubt the greatest enthusiast!) Suzan was always delighted when I told her I was going to play golf. Her eyes would light up, and she would say with a smile, "Oh, Dad, I'm so glad! You need to play more golf. You have so much fun on the course!" On the rare occasions when I was able to play with Chad, she seemed particularly delighted.

On that day, Chad, Richard, Tom, and I formed a team. We play respectively to handicaps of 21, 18, 4, and 14. In other words, we were not a quartet of high-performance golfers. We were playing "best ball," which means that each person in the foursome hits each shot and then the best shot is used as the starting point for the next round of four shots. In this form of the game, the final score is always lower than any one golfer's score. On that day, we did well, and we came in with an amazing best-ball score of 57.

The chances of that happening among the four of us even on a good day of golf were somewhere between slim and none. The round was almost funny at times because on several of the holes, three of us would foul up completely and then the fourth one would hit a genuine hero shot— perhaps sinking a twenty-five-foot putt, making an impossible shot from under a tree, or killing a drive. In one case, Chad hit a drive of more than three hundred yards. Then Richard, Tom, and I proceeded to butcher our sixty-yard approach shots to the pin, but Chad stepped up with his sand wedge, lofted the ball high in the air, and dropped it about ten feet from the pin, and it rolled in from there! I said to myself while the ball was still in the air, "That's going to be close." When it landed, I thought, *Real close*. As it continued to roll toward the pin, I thought, *Real, REAL close!* And then it disappeared into the hole.

If you are not a golfer, you probably cannot appreciate how excited I was by that particular round of golf. On the day I hit a 7-wood 170 yards and knocked it into the hole for an eagle, or even on August 8, 1997, when I hit a 151-yard hole in one, bystanders must have thought I had just been handed the key to Fort Knox. However, when Chad scored his eagle, everyone in our foursome responded with intense joy and enthusiasm, displayed by a loud round of cheering! I suspect everyone on the golf course knew something *big* had happened. And so it is that I can say without any mental reservation whatsoever—having known both disastrous rounds of golf and an exhilarating one that had a hole-in-one shot—I had more fun on the golf course for that Prestonwood golf and tennis day than I have ever had on a golf course in my life.

My son, Tom, won the putting contest. I won the "closest to the hole" contest on one of the holes. Each one of us on the Ziglar team won a hundred-dollar gift certificate at the pro shop for having the low score of the day, our stellar 57. It was truly a magnificent occasion, and I am convinced that the day was a gift from God. I believe He wanted each of us to have an opportunity to relax, put our minds toward something other than our grief, and have a good time. That day was yet a further sign of assurance to me that we have a loving, yes, even fun-loving, God who likes to see His children enjoy His creation to the fullest.

We all speculated, of course, about whether Suzan's presence in heaven had anything to do with our spectacular shots and our delightful day. I do know with certainty that if Suzan had been present with us on the course that day, she would have been just as excited about our game as we were. She loved to see people have fun.

Did I experience joy that day on the golf course with my family? Yes, indeed. Was it a miracle gift of God to me less than two weeks after the saddest day of my life? Absolutely.

GOD REMINDS US OF HIS PRESENT HELP

Shortly after Suzan's funeral, Cindy, Julie, and their mother went to Suzan's house to go through her closet and to make proper disposition of her clothing. In the process they came across some photographs taken of Suzan when she had visited Cindy and Richard in Sacramento. The pictures brought back many beautiful memories to Cindy, and knowing that she had made a second copy of the photographs for herself, she wanted to find them as soon as she returned home later that day.

According to Cindy, however, her thousands of photographs were "in complete disarray." As she started to search for the particular photos, she prayed, "Lord, I so badly want to find those pictures. Will You guide me directly to them?"

The first box she pulled from the storage area contained the very photos she was seeking! Coincidence? In Cindy's conviction, one I share, a loving God had manifested Himself once again in a way that brought about peace and assurance of His love for us and His concern with the little things of our lives. His miracle moment to Cindy was a sharp reminder that He is present with us always and that no detail of our lives is too small for His concern.

ALL THINGS *ARE* WORKING TOGETHER FOR GOD'S GOOD

At our Christmas party in December of 1996, we invited about seventy friends and staff members to join us for a buffet-style dinner and the exchange of inexpensive Christmas ornaments. After the exchange of gifts, Thelma Wells, one of our contract speakers, led us in singing Christmas carols. Thelma's voice is so spectacular that I moved around to her side as the group was singing and asked her if she knew "Sweet Little Jesus Boy." She said yes, she'd be pleased to sing it, and a little later in the evening, she did. When she hit the line, "We didn't know who You was," I felt a surge of emotion. For the first forty-five years of my life, I didn't know who He was. His entrance into my life brought about the most complete transformation I believe a human being can experience. I was filled with gratefulness once again for the Lord's love and forgiveness.

Was it a coincidence that Thelma knew that song? Thelma told me later that she had not sung that song in more than twenty years, but that very morning God had put it on her heart to rehearse "Sweet Little Jesus Boy." She even found herself praying that God might make it possible for her to sing that song for me that evening. She had no way of knowing how much I love that song or what it means to me. There is no way anyone could convince me that her beautiful rendition of this old spiritual was a coincidence. I believe a loving God looked down, saw His hurting child, and said, "I believe My son would love to hear this song tonight."

Thelma did not know that earlier that evening, before the meal, I had mentioned to my wife and daughter Cindy that my only regret about the coming party was that I had not arranged for someone to sing "Sweet Little Jesus Boy." I hadn't, but God had.

I believe in our periods of deepest grief, we can trust God to prepare someone to come our way to speak a word of love or encouragement to us, or perhaps to be present with us, to weep with us, or to walk with us in silence and faith. He may compel a church choir leader to choose just the right anthem for you to hear, or He may inspire your pastor to speak just the right words that will spark in you the faith you need to get you through your time of intense pain. We worship a great God. He loves us and prepares for us the comfort we need in our grief.

God's miracle moments are reminders that He is orchestrating a grand plan for our eternal benefit. All things, large and small, are being fitted together for the greater good that He has created for us.

As you grieve, don't miss the miracle moments that God will surely send *your* way. Recognize His hand at work. Accept His gifts of joy to you as you see not coincidences, but blessings and miracles.

10

COMFORT AND JOY
FROM PRAYER AND
THE WORD

AFTER A LIGHT breakfast that first morning after Suzan's death, my wife and I talked, cried, and did our best to console each other. Then I went out for a walk. I had not expected it to be the glorious experience that it turned out to be. It was almost as if I were walking with God Himself as He opened Himself up to me in a new way during that next hour of my life.

On my walk, I think I wept more and harder over a longer period of time than I have ever wept before or since in my entire life. I asked God to allow me to feel His presence, His comfort, and His assurance that Suzan was well. Even though I already believed that in my mind, I wanted to *feel* God's assurance in my heart.

I prayed for each member of our family on that walk, that the experience of loss would bring us even closer together and that we would have the strength to deal with our grief as strongly and effectively as Suzan had dealt with her impending death.

While Suzan undoubtedly regretted leaving her family and she fully understood the impact her departure would have on us, her faith in God also assured her that she would be all right and *we* (including her children) would be all right. God had given her a peace that allowed her to pass into eternity with a calm and yet exhilarating faith. As I walked, I prayed for that same peace and comfort to fill my heart.

I also asked God for guidance and direction. From the very first day of my grieving, I wanted God to be in the center of my grief. I wanted Him to guide me into the things that would be most helpful and healing to me. Certainly He has answered this prayer and continues to answer it. On that walk, God's answer for peace and guidance *began*.

In my continued tears on that first day after Suzan's death, God began to impress a number of things on my heart in a way that enabled me to truly feel His presence moving in me. As I neared the house, He assured me that Suzan was fine, that she was with Him, and that He was all I needed. He impressed me that crying and praying were exactly what I needed to do and that I should continue to walk and pray and weep in the days ahead. He gave me the assurance, far more clearly than I can express on these pages, that He would be with me and each member of my family and see to it that our lives would continue forward and our faith would continue to grow. That was precisely the assurance I needed for that day.

GOD SPEAKS TO US THROUGH LIVING PARABLES

On the second day after Suzan's death, I again went on a walk to talk with God. Again, I walked and cried and prayed.

I knew I was in obedience to what God had told me to do on my walk the previous morning.

During that particular walk, my thoughts turned to how God might use the occasion of Suzan's death and funeral to claim the souls of nonbelievers for the kingdom, to alleviate the grief of our family, and to clarify some of the promises of God for those who were unsaved or even baby or immature Christians. On that second walk, the idea for this book came to my mind.

Then my thoughts turned to Psalm 23. I thought of the still waters mentioned in this psalm, and suddenly I reversed my direction and walked over to the lake, which is about a quarter of a mile from our home. As I approached the lake, my first view of it was that the waters, indeed, were still, quiet, and peaceful. I prayed that God would give me a peace in my heart that was just like the still peace He had created for the lake that morning. Getting closer to the lake, I noticed an ugly plastic bag, partially opened and displaying garbage, including many beer cans. My thought was, *How tragic when we in society dump so much garbage on God's handiwork and onto God's people.* I determined that I would let nothing dump negative thoughts, images, or feelings into my spirit.

As I continued on my walk around the lake, a duck jumped into the water and quickly swam away. I thought, *Here is life in its fullest. This is part of God's plan. We are to be active, even in the stillness God gives to us.* Then I looked out into the lake and noticed a turtle's head sticking above the water. I recalled that just three days earlier my son and I had talked about the fact that some types of turtles are predators of baby ducklings. I thought of the fact that Satan preys on Christians, always lurking just beneath the surface of our lives, anxious to pull us down and drown us by one means or another. I quickly resolved that I would try to communicate to others that we must be forever on the alert against the wiles of Satan, the father of lies.

Farther around the lake, I saw two beautiful doves take off in full flight. At that point I thought, *That's what God permits us to do when we trust Him. He helps us to rise above the challenges of life and to fly to Him for the comfort, strength, wisdom, and solutions to problems that we need.* I couldn't help rejoicing. Truly we serve a great God!

What a wonderful set of parables God gave to me that morning as I walked and talked and wept and reflected upon His Word and His goodness to me. A walk that began in sadness ended in joy.

GOD GIVES US HIS INSIGHTS AND GUIDES OUR PRAYERS

On yet another day as I was walking and praying, I pondered the magnitude of the impact that words have had on my life. The Bible says that God spoke the world into existence. His words have certainly given my world new meaning. I prayed that God's Word would give new meaning to my granddaughter Katherine's life and that His Word would have a powerful impact on her.

I explained to God during my "walking prayer" all the things He already knew—that Katherine was only fifteen, that she had lost the mother who loved her deeply and understood her better than anyone and on whom she had depended so much. Through an avalanche of tears, I asked God to help Katherine understand what had happened in a way that would make her know that God is God and that He loves her mother more by far than she did, that everything

He does is in our long-range best interests, and that everything He does is motivated by His love for her.

I wept as I prayed and walked, knowing the pain and the hurt that Katherine was going through because she missed her mother, knowing her need for a loving God.

I recalled an incident at the hospital when the Redhead could see how distraught Katherine was and how desperately she was trying to get close to her mother. She encouraged Katherine to climb onto the hospital bed and lie by her mother's side. Katherine did that and stayed there for some time, crying and holding the mother she loved so dearly. At one point during Suzan's hospital stay, Katherine asked the question that was ripping out our hearts: "What will I do without her?"

As I continued to walk and pray, my mind drifted to my childhood and scenes of my mother, who had only a fifth-grade education and who found herself a widow during the heart of the depression with six children too young to work. My mother used to sing "The Old Rugged Cross" on the back porch while she churned butter from the milk she got from our five milk cows. To this day, when anyone sings "The Old Rugged Cross," I weep tears of gratitude for my mother who was filled with an incredible amount of faith, love, and courage. I remember going to Wednesday night prayer meetings with my mother and hearing her sing in her clear voice "Sweet Hour of Prayer." When I hear anyone sing "Sweet Hour of Prayer" today, I am flooded with memories of my mother.

On my walk, I began to pray for Chad. I realized the immediacy of the loss he must feel in his daily life. As he took on the unfamiliar tasks of providing meals and making certain that various things in the household were running smoothly, I knew he missed Suzan in ways he had not imagined. I realized Chad's need for God's love at this time. I prayed and wept while asking God to give Chad special patience and communication skills with Katherine, who needed his guidance, his presence, his love, and his assurance more than ever. I prayed God would give Chad the wisdom to handle all of the family responsibilities thrust upon him so unexpectedly.

The ability to take my needs to God in prayer helped me not to feel entirely helpless in the face of my loss. Praying gives me a sense that I have some control over how I respond to my feelings and future. Talking to God about the needs of my family and asking Him to help them kept me from feeling alone in my grief. I may not be able to control anything other than how and when I communicate with God, but in the end, that is enough.

Words of prayer are the most effective words of all. They are the basis of our ongoing walk of faith and our relationship with our loving heavenly Father.

A COMPANION FOR MY WALKS

There was yet another lesson that I learned through my daily prayer walks with the Lord—a parable of sorts that is ongoing.

For thousands of years, ministers have proclaimed to their congregations, "God works in mysterious ways." One of the greatest mysteries to me has been the way God has used a little Welsh corgi to bring me comfort in my grief.

Cindy enjoys her dog, Emmitt, so much that for months prior to Suzan's death, she and her sister Julie had embarked upon a plot to get a dog into our house. The two girls set out to persuade their mother that a dog would provide company for her when I was traveling, and as part of their plot, they took her to a dog show. There, the Redhead saw Welsh corgis in action and fell in love with them.

I wasn't at all sure that acquiring a dog was a good idea, but within five minutes after Laffy Taffy walked through the door into our home, he had also walked straight into our hearts, mine included. I nicknamed him Dirty Dog, and we have been big buddies ever since. This all occurred about three months before Suzan's death.

Dirty Dog has been an entertaining distraction in times when grief and sadness weighed heavily on me. He has gone on walks with me, and he has made me laugh over his insistent way of getting me to chase him around the house or throw toys for him to retrieve. Dirty Dog has been a fun-filled companion, offering the Redhead and me comforting love and total acceptance. In the grieving process, these things are very helpful.

I believe that if you will permit God to do so, He will put something or someone in your life who will

- create a *necessity* for shifting gears occasionally away from grief and toward gratitude and opportunities to laugh.

- love you and accept you with unconditional love.

- cause you to connect in a very real way with the mundane and ordinary chores and pleasures of life.

- give you reason to laugh at life's many foibles and oddities.

He will answer the unspoken prayer request of your heart in ways you haven't yet imagined.

THE GREAT COMFORT FOUND
IN GOD'S WORD

Beyond the comfort I have found in my prayer walks with God is that which I have found in my daily encounter with God's Word. There truly is no substitute for the power of God's Word to bring healing and joy into our lives.

Many years ago someone said that one picture is worth ten thousand words. As I have said in many talks and books, the person who said that had obviously never read the Bill of Rights or the Declaration of Independence. He certainly had not read the Twenty-third Psalm or prayed the Lord's Prayer. He most likely had never read Lincoln's "Gettysburg Address" or a host of other literary masterpieces that have inspired mankind since the beginning of time. All of those documents are words—*just words*—but they have changed the lives of untold millions of people.

In my lifetime, I have experienced joy and grief and the life-changing impact of the spoken word.

On September 15, 1944, I met a beautiful sixteen-year-old high school girl and was enormously attracted to her. Her name was Jean Abernathy, and not too many weeks after I met her, I said to her, "I love you." A few months later she said to me, "I love you too." Those words excited and pleased me enormously. A little more than two years after I met her, a preacher said, "I now pronounce you man and wife," and the two of us undertook a tumultuous, exciting, loving, and sometimes difficult journey.

Words impact our lives. The Holy Spirit used words to bring Suzan to the point of accepting Jesus Christ as her Savior. In the minutes and days immediately after Suzan died, the pastors who were present—Jim Lewis, John West, Michael FinCannon, and Jack Graham—repeatedly said to us things that we already knew to be true but that we needed to hear: "Suzan is no longer in pain," "Suzan now lives in a perfect heavenly body," and "Suzan is at home with the Lord." These words had an impact on us. They brought us comfort and hope. Words were used at Suzan's funeral service to comfort and reassure everyone who loved her.

As valuable as the words of loved ones and friends may be to us in our grief, however, no words are more potent or have more meaning than God's Word. Throughout the grieving process, something that kept coming back to me in seemingly a hundred and one different ways was the truth of the richness of God's promises. For example, Isaiah 49:15 (NLT) asks, "Can a mother forget her nursing child? Can she feel no love for a child she has borne?" God answers by saying, "But even if that were possible, I would not forget you!" To those who grieve, what a comfort it is to be assured that God fully understands our feelings and knows our needs. I believe one reason God sent Christ to this earth was to show us that God fully understands all that we feel and experience on this earth.

SPEAKING GOD'S WORD ALOUD

For some time, especially during my grieving process, I have been heavily involved in biblical self-talk. I have always found this to be an exciting and encouraging way of reading God's promises. I take God's Word and translate it into a first-person, present-tense form, which I speak aloud.

One morning my schedule of Bible reading called for me to read Psalm 46 and Psalm 47. I found these verses enormously encouraging. Psalm 46:1 (NKJV), for example, says, "God is our refuge and strength, a very present help in trouble." I spoke it aloud in this way: "God is *my* refuge and strength, a very present help in my time of trouble." Trouble refers to all kinds of trouble, including the troubled heart that a grieving person feels.

I spoke Psalm 46:2–6 in this way:

> *Therefore I will not fear, even though the earth is removed, and though the mountains are carried into the midst of the sea; though its waters roar and are troubled, though the mountains shake with its swelling. There is a river whose streams shall make glad the city of God—including Suzan who lives there—the holy place of the tabernacle of the Most High. God is in the midst of her, she shall not be moved; and neither will I be moved in my trust and faith.*

Powerful comfort comes to me in speaking aloud the Scriptures in this way. On occasion, I have shouted with joy as I have praised the Lord for the goodness He reveals in His Word.

Stop to think for a moment about what it means that a river of *joy* flows through the city of God where God lives. Suzan experiences that joy daily. It is the same joy that I can experience. And in a wonderful and mysterious way, I find it incredibly comforting and exciting to think that Suzan and I can both drink from the same flow of God's joy!

Psalm 47:1–4 (NKJV) tells us,

> *Oh, clap your hands, all you peoples!*
> *Shout to God with the voice of triumph!*
> *For the LORD Most High is awesome;*
> *He is a great King over all the earth.*
> *He will subdue the peoples under us,*
> *And the nations under our feet.*

He will choose our inheritance for us,
The excellence of Jacob whom He loves.

What a wonderful feeling filled my heart as I spoke these words in this way: "I clap my hands (which I did)—I shout to God with a voice that says, 'We're winning! You are awesome, Lord. You are my King. You are subduing all circumstances and all nations under Your feet. You have chosen me for a great inheritance. You are planning for me the very best of all that You have because I love You.'" How easy it was to imagine Suzan in heaven clapping her hands and then saying in her voice, "I've won, in Christ! Lord, You are awesome. You have given me a great inheritance, the very best of everything!"

I have no doubt that Suzan is praising and worshiping God with all of her being in heaven. And what words will she use in praise if not the *eternal* words of God's Book? The Scriptures teach us that the Word of God is eternal; it does not change and it lasts forever. The words that give me sustaining hope and joy and peace on this earth are the same words that are to be found in Suzan's praises to her Savior and Lord.

A few minutes after I had finished reading the Scriptures during my morning devotional hour, I went downstairs and greeted my wife, who as always returned the big hug I gave her. Then as we sat down to breakfast, I prayed, "Thank You, Lord, for this day You have given us. I know it is the one You have made for us, and we are going to rejoice and be glad in it." Even without thinking it, I was praying Psalm 118:24.

As I concluded my prayer, the Redhead looked at me and said, "I needed that. I have not been having a good morning." We chatted for a moment, and I shared further with her the blessing that Psalms 46–47 had been to me that morning. We both left the breakfast table with hopeful hearts.

Let me share how I "translated" yet another passage of Scripture into the first person. It is Psalm 84:5–6, which I recite in this way: "When Suzan went home to be with the Lord and I walked through the valley of weeping, it became a place of springs filled with pools of blessing and refreshing."

Time and again in the midst of my grieving process, these verses have been true for me. There have been times when I know without a doubt that God gave me extra strength and insights into how I might conduct my work and live my life, and even more important, there have been times when I have experienced a heightened sensitivity to the hurts and needs of others.

Pools of blessing and refreshing can come in the form of new ideas. One day as I was walking and praying and thinking and meditating after a period of sorrow and weeping, this thought came to mind: *Knowledge, founded on truth, gives power. Motivation is the switch that releases the power and converts it into active wisdom.* That idea has given me much to dwell on in the subsequent years. It was a capsule idea that truly became an ongoing pool of blessing and refreshing.

GOD GIVES US *DAILY* HELP

In sharing my prayer walk and Bible-reading experiences with you, I want to convey to you that the Lord throughout His Book calls us to a daily walk of faith and trust in Him.

On my daily walk, I express my needs to the Lord, and He reveals Himself to me in unusual and encouraging ways.

In my daily Bible reading, I express my praise to God, and the Lord reveals to me His daily provision.

On my walk and in speaking the Scriptures aloud, I express to the Lord where I am in my grieving, and He, in turn, provides for me the insight, joy, and help that I need to be healed and made stronger in my faith.

My trust grows daily. And that truly seems to be the way God has designed our spiritual growth. He does not take us by leaps and bounds from one level of spiritual maturity to another; rather, He leads us step-by-step into the way we should go and into the depths of His love and care.

Our healing from grief to a very great extent lies in our *daily* communication with the Lord.

11

WE GRIEVE IN
DIFFERENT WAYS

GRIEF IS AN intensely personal thing, and different people handle it in vastly different ways.

Some take comfort in leaving items in their homes just as they were when the loved one died. Sometimes they won't move—or permit anyone else to move—anything, even for years. Others clean out all reminders of the loved one in fairly short order.

Soon after Suzan's death, Chad asked Cindy and Julie to help him clean out many of Suzan's personal possessions, such as clothing and makeup. That action had nothing to do with his love for Suzan. His love for her and his grief over his loss are deep and evident, and will always be a part of him, just as our love and grief will be parts of the rest of us. He expressed his grief, however, in his own way, and we supported him completely in his grief process.

In comparison, Cindy had an absolute passion for finding every remnant that connected her to Suzan. She searched out all the photographs, letters, notes, and various items associated with times they had spent together. She was almost obsessed with immersing herself in memoirs of all of the things in which Suzan had participated or in which they had shared as sisters. Again, we encouraged Cindy to express her grief in the way she chose.

I have partly dealt with my grief by keeping a journal. The journal has been a very helpful and healing outlet for me. At times I wrote in it almost on a daily basis. Thoughts of Suzan were ever present, and words about her flowed freely. Through my journal keeping, I was able to gain perspective on life and our loss. That journal has been the basis on which this book was written.

WHAT CAUSES COMFORT TO ONE MAY CAUSE PAIN TO ANOTHER

Our family members have dealt differently with grief in relation to photographs of Suzan. Cindy carries a picture of Suzan in a locket she wears constantly. She and Julie often look through photos they have of Suzan. I initially found looking at photos of Suzan very painful, even though writing about her was not always painful.

Chad gave us a particular photograph of Suzan. It is one of the few close-up snapshots we have of her, and Chad was kind enough to have enlargements of the photo made for everyone in the family. It is a beautiful photograph, taken on her last visit to California to see Cindy and Richard. We hung it in our kitchen. I simply could not look at that photograph, however, for about two months following Suzan's death. The photo was so much like her—so alive—that it brought a flood of tears each time I saw it, so I avoided looking at it.

Several times, photographs have triggered tears and

deep sadness in me. Just three months after Suzan's death, the Redhead gave me a small, beautiful photograph of Suzan, and she said, "This can go on your bedside table." I couldn't help thinking, *I miss my little girl.* A week or so later, the Redhead found some negatives that included a picture of our three daughters. Suzan was in the center with her arms around her sisters, and they were laughing and showing off the earrings they had received that Christmas. Suzan was laughing the hardest, and she appeared to be the happiest of the three. Although I didn't notice it at first, Julie later pointed out to me that Suzan had the biggest smile because she had her hands behind her sisters' heads with her fingers sticking up to look like bunny ears! As I looked closer, I both laughed and wept. I couldn't help thinking, *I miss that laugh.*

Visual images as a whole seemed to be a surefire way to bring up memories that resulted in tears and sorrow. *Why is this?* I wondered.

I finally had to face the fact that the last visual image I had in my mind was of Suzan's body at the funeral home. That image of my daughter flashed back into my mind most often when I thought about her. I decided that the image was *not* the one I wanted to carry with me. I worked diligently at replacing that image with images of Suzan on the happy occasions we had together. Most, but not all, of the images I have of Suzan are drawn from my happy memories and not photographs.

DON'T EXPECT GRIEF TO BE LOGICAL

Some people desire to often visit the graves of their departed loved ones. Others don't feel the need. Some feel comforted in visiting the cemetery where they buried their loved ones. Others experience more grief in visiting a grave site.

While the Redhead and I understand clearly that Suzan is not in the cemetery—only the mortal remains of her physical body are there—we find ourselves thinking of a visit to the cemetery as a visit to Suzan. We have a need to go to the grave site periodically to express our grief. We know that this is not logical, but grief isn't logical! We need to allow for that fact as others around us grieve. We need to expect grief to be illogical.

ALLOW FOR CONTRADICTIONS

If you are grieving the loss of a loved one, don't be surprised that there are seeming contradictions in the way you handle your grief, or that the way you handle your grief seems to change over time. God deals with each of us differently, and no single way of expressing grief is good, better, or best. Rather, the way we handle or express grief is simply the way *we* handle or express grief. No person can tell you what the best way is for *you* to respond to the loss of someone you love.

One of the mysteries about grief and death involves the events that frequently occur once the funeral has been completed, and close friends and family members gather together. They gather to celebrate the homegoing of a loved one and also to support the family members in their grief. Friends and members of the church family nearly always provide food. If a stranger from another planet suddenly dropped in on one of these occasions, he would see little indication that those in attendance had just been to an emotional ceremony in which the body of a lost loved one was committed to the grave. It would be hard to explain why so much laughter was expressed at the postfuneral gathering, much less why jokes were being told or why people were discussing everything from football games to the stock market. These gatherings, however, are also a part of the grieving process. The emotions related to the trauma of the loss, the intensity of the funeral service, and the finality that a loved one is no longer present with us on earth need some form of closure and release. In some cases the mere fact that the funeral is over brings closure to the finality of the loss and consequently a sense of relief.

Knowing Suzan as I do, I feel certain that she would have wanted laughter to dominate the gathering after her funeral. As a matter of fact, from her perspective she was off to the biggest party of all; therefore, a party was certainly in order as a final tribute to her and her "graduation."

DON'T TRY TO CONTROL
HOW OTHERS GRIEVE

As the first Christmas without Suzan approached, I had a feeling of dread in my heart. Holiday celebrations, which are always family times for us, seemed to be some of the most difficult times of grieving for me. I could hardly imagine what that first Christmas would be like. A family tradition was for all of us to go to Suzan's house on Christmas night. Suzan cooked a big meal, and Chad, Katherine, and Elizabeth joined her in entertaining us royally. We could count on Suzan's laughter filling the house.

In October, Katherine informed Cindy that she and Chad had been talking about Christmas and that they were planning once again to host this occasion. In fact, they had already decided what to prepare for dinner.

My first impulse was to say, *Oh, no, you can't do that.* And then I caught myself. I realized that I had come very close to making a big mistake—of making a decision for others when I should trust them to make their own decisions. From my perspective, what they were about to do would cause them pain. And yet, from their perspective, what they were planning did not seem to be causing them pain and in fact was part of their healing process.

HOW, THEN, SHALL WE GRIEVE?

If there are no sct patterns to grief, and if grief is so highly unpredictable and illogical, what can we say about *how* to grieve?

First, I encourage you to acknowledge that you are grieving. Do not attempt to deny, avoid, or put off feelings of sadness. I have admitted I am a grieving Christian. My heart is broken. Yet because I have given all the broken pieces to Christ, as Mary Crowley advised everyone to do, He is healing my heart and assuring me daily that Suzan is with Him and she is well.

Second, allow the grief process to run its full course in your life. Psychologists have written that the major portion of grief usually runs about a two-year course and that one never fully gets over feelings of grief. To deny or attempt to shorten the grieving process is to find yourself in even greater pain for longer periods of time. It also permits the entrance of bitterness and despair.

"We must get on with life" is an empty comment, yet it is one that is nearly always stated. While it is true that we

must get on with our lives, any implication that we will forget the loved one is absurd. There is no magic moment
when you move from sadness and sorrow to a total lack of
sadness and sorrow. There is no magic formula that will
instantly make all of the pain go away.

Grieving is a process that takes time, there are no short-
cuts. It also takes the love and encouragement of family
members and friends. There is no proper mourning period
as many people have proclaimed through the years.
Grieving is a highly individualized process. The timetable
you experience may not be the same as that of others,
including close family members.

I have found that time becomes a bit warped in grief. At
times throughout the first holiday season after Suzan's
death, I reflected on several occasions that it seemed to
have been an eternity since Suzan went home to be with the
Lord, and yet at other moments during that same holiday
season, it seemed to have been only yesterday that we were
making funeral arrangements.

How long does grief last? I have no idea. Every person's
situation is different. Some people tell me that twenty-five
years after the death of a loved one, they are still grieving. I
feel certain that the intensity of grief lessens over time and
that for most people with whom I've talked, intense grief
seems to be limited to the first year or two after the person's
death. There is a dramatic difference in the intensity and
duration of the grief I've felt over the passing of my parents
or even my siblings, compared to the deep grief I have felt
over the loss of my daughter.

Those who may say to you, with all good intentions, "It's
time to put this behind you," or "You need to straighten up
now," or "Get hold of yourself," may be well meaning, but
they don't have a clue about what it means to go through

the process of grieving that is essential for healing to take place in God's timing.

The simple but sure truth is that each of us deals with grief in a different way and on a different timetable.

To a great extent, you will walk this journey on your own. Although this may not be a comforting thought to you, I trust that you will find comfort in knowing that the process is one that the *Lord* is guiding and directing in your life, and the *Lord* is walking every step of this journey with you. He made you to be a totally unique creation, including a unique creation in your grief. He completely understands the grieving process you are experiencing, and He will be with you through the entire process—regardless of its length and intensity.

12

COMFORTING THE GRIEVING

WHAT IS MOST helpful to the grieving person? What brings the greatest comfort? If I were to make a suggestion to friends of the family that has lost a loved one, I would say this: "Let the grieving person know that *you* know he is hurting."

You can be present to listen to the grieving person talk about whatever he wishes. Many times the grieving person simply needs to *talk*—not to receive advice or to invite memories from the other person, but to relate emotions and share thoughts. Don't be hesitant or embarrassed at initiating times to sit quietly or be present for the grieving person.

Some people tend to literally discount the child who has departed. Both the Redhead and I have experienced times in which people refer to our three children. The fact is that we have *four* children—three living on this earth and one in heaven. Our fourth child is no less our child. She is no less a member of our family. The name of the lost loved

141

one is not a secret. Be willing to speak the name of the person who is no longer physically with you.

HUGS CAN HELP HEAL

Time and again, friends have helped my wife and me in the grieving process with the comforting therapy of hugs. I recall vividly the very timely hugs given to me by Lisa McInnis-Smith when she and her family were visiting with us a couple of months after Suzan died; the hug that John West, our associate pastor, gave us after he saw us weeping in response to the hymn "Because He Lives"; the hug from Charlie Brown, who saw the Redhead and me in our grief and came to us and asked if we were all right. Beyond the timeliness and spontaneity of the compassion these friends extended to us, I was impressed that each of them asked us if they could hug us, or they volunteered a hug with the utmost respect for our feelings. At no time was there any sense that they were violating our space or invading our privacy. They were sensitive to our needs, and they sensed that we needed the hugs they offered so freely.

Sometimes giving a quick hug and just being present speak volumes to the grieving person. Answers are not the key; your presence is what counts. Make your presence felt.

You don't necessarily need to say anything when you give a person a hug. One long-standing friend, who was particularly close to Suzan, on a number of occasions has simply grabbed my hand or hugged the Redhead or me. Nothing is said, although tears are often shed.

In the spring 1996 issue of *The Grapevine,* a publication

of Don Anderson Ministries, Dan and Cay Bolin were inter-
viewed about how they dealt with their daughter Catie's illness with leukemia, her death, and the grief that followed.
The answers to interviewer Jane Rodger's question, "What
advice would you offer those who wish to help others in similar circumstances?" expressed my sentiments so well that I
am going to quote their answers in full:

> DAN: Be sensitive but available. Some friends were so
> afraid of intruding upon our family time that they
> avoided calling us or asking us to do things as they
> had before. Other folks felt compelled to start a
> relationship with us, but in truth, we didn't have
> energy for new friendships. Send food, do practical
> things to help, but keep the friendship at the same
> level as before. If you've been meeting with some-
> one once a week for prayer, keep on doing it. If your
> acquaintance has been casual, a crisis is not the time
> to try to deepen it. You want to be surrounded by
> people who have been close to you.

> CAY: Don't avoid talking about the person who has
> died. I love it when the mother of Catie's best friend
> recalls things Catie said or did. I realize Catie was
> important to her, too. It helps when people remem-
> ber and call or send cards on special dates. Every
> October 4, Catie's birthday, someone places a
> pumpkin on her grave site. We don't know who
> does it, but it means a lot.

If you trust God and ask Him to direct you in the way
you comfort the grieving, you can relax in the knowledge
that His will is being done.

PRAYING FOR THOSE WHO GRIEVE

Many people have said to me in the months and years since Suzan died, "I am praying for you." I find immense comfort in that loving statement.

When people tell me that they are praying for me outside the context of my grief, I always ask them to pray for three specific things: first, that God will give me wisdom so that I will know what to do; second, that God will make me humble so that He might use me; third, that God will give me the courage to do what needs to be done and say what needs to be said.

I truly believe that God gives us not only His love, strength, mercy, and power, but also the "mind of Christ." (See 1 Cor. 2:16.) I am confident that God frequently takes us into His inner sanctum and makes us His confidants so that He might share His wisdom with us. (See Pss. 19:7; 25:14.) I have deeply desired from God the wisdom about how to grieve.

When you pray for another person, I encourage you to pray love, strength, and wisdom for him. If you have the privilege to pray with him face-to-face, I recommend a prayer that speaks of God's love, power, and guidance.

WHAT MIGHT YOU SAY?

I have encountered a number of people who have admitted to me that they do not know *how* to comfort the grieving members of families who have lost a loved one. I encourage them first and foremost to be sensitive to the person who is grieving. A sensitivity to emotions and needs is far more important than any specific words that are spoken or written.

A message that is always welcome to the grieving person

is actually very simple: "I'm sorry. I'm praying for you. I really care."

With a short letter my friend John Maxwell and his wife, Margaret, comforted and encouraged us after Suzan died. I share it with their permission:

To Zig and Jean,

Today I am flying into Dallas to attend the funeral service of your daughter. Your entire family has been continually in my prayers since I heard the sad news from Margaret. You have many friends that want to give you love and support. Margaret and I want to be counted among them.

Zig, over the last few years we have enjoyed many good times together. Today I want to share grief with you and Jean over the loss of your daughter. I offer to you my continued love, friendship, and prayers.

For the Christian, death does not end with a period or a question mark. It ends with a comma, life continues with God. May God's sustaining grace continue to be yours.

Love,

John and Margaret Maxwell

The very best ways to comfort others are astoundingly simple. My friend in this letter offered us continued love, friendship, and prayers. What else is there? He gave us the very best support anyone can give. And he did it on an ordinary sheet of notebook paper, blue lines and all.

Samuel Henning, pastor of Abundant Life Christian Center in Alton, Illinois, and father of Jill Henning, one of our outstanding salespeople, sent us a very comforting letter.

He included a story that had touched him at a family friend's memorial service two years earlier. Printed on his friend's memorial pamphlet were the following words by an anonymous author:

Gone from My Sight

I am standing upon the seashore. A ship at my side spreads her white sails to the morning breeze and starts for the blue ocean. She is an object of beauty and strength. I stand and watch her until at length she hangs like a cloud just where the sea and sky come to mingle with each other.

Then someone at my side says, "There, she is gone!"

Gone where?

Gone from my sight. That is all. She is just as large in mast and spar as she was when she left my side and she is just as able to bear her load of living freight to her destined port.

Her diminished size is in me, not in her. And just at the moment when someone at my side says, "There, she is gone!" there are eyes watching her coming, and other voices ready to take up the glad shout, "Here she comes!"—and that is dying.

Pastor Henning closed his letter by saying, "Our hearts reach out to comfort you . . . Our prayers reach heaven to carry you in God's grace . . . and our friendship is ever available to you to lift your burden in tender sharing. In Christ's love and comfort, Samuel."

Beautifully written, caring thoughts shared with us in our time of all-consuming grief lifted us in indescribable ways. I feel certain that when John Maxwell and Samuel Henning picked up their pens to write to us, they did not yet know what they would write. I believe God gave them the words they used because they were the words I needed to read, and God knows my needs and sees that they are met.

IT'S NEVER TOO LATE TO
WRITE CONDOLENCES

John Maxwell wrote his condolence letter on his way to attend our daughter's funeral. Samuel Henning wrote his letter on February 2, 1996, almost nine months after Suzan died. Both men had perfect timing. Don't ever think that it is inappropriate to mention a lost loved one simply because time has passed. Believe me—folks are still grieving months and years after their loss, and most people welcome the opportunity to revisit memories of their loved ones and to receive expressions of heartfelt love and concern.

A few weeks before her death, Suzan received a beautiful angel card from her cousin, Carol Ann Melton. She loved that card—its concept and message were beautiful. Suzan's sister Cindy had fully intended to take the card to the hospital to place it on the wall where Suzan could see it, but in the turmoil and anxiety associated with Suzan's hospital stay, Cindy forgot to do so. A few days after the funeral, Cindy's friend Kelsey Hall sent her the very same card, and it was a beautiful and thoughtful encouragement to Cindy. Such a little thing, yet it was a meaningful moment to Cindy to receive precisely the same card. You never can tell how much your words and actions of encouragement may mean to someone in grief.

A REMINDER OF WHAT WE
BELIEVE AS CHRISTIANS

In a beautiful handwritten note from Dina and Jack Landers, who had recently lost their precious two-year-old son, Dina pointed out these comforting words from Isaiah 61:2–3 (NLT): "He has sent me to tell those who mourn that the time of the LORD's favor has come, and with it, the day of God's anger against their enemies. To all who mourn in Israel, he will give beauty for ashes, joy instead of mourning, praise instead of despair. For the LORD has planted them like strong and graceful oaks for his own glory." Then Dina went on to say that she and Jack were comforted by these promises of the Lord. She further pointed out that in death, her son Aubrey achieved more than many people will accomplish in a hundred years of life. And how right she was! Dina shared the beauty and strength of her faith, saying, "I do not have all the answers. I don't need them. I know that my God who dwells in the heavens has a perfect plan for my life, for Aubrey's life, for us all."

What Dina expressed is what my family and I also feel about Suzan. We were comforted at being reminded of what we *believe.*

The incredible support I received from so many Christian brothers and sisters helped make my grief bearable. In many cases, they reminded me of the goodness of God's Word.

Don Hawkins, an avid Bible student and a man of real love and compassion, sent me a telegram in which he reminded me of Psalm 116:15 (TLB), which tells us that God's loved ones are very precious to Him and He does not "lightly let them die." Our Savior knows our feelings. He walked on this earth as a human being and experienced all

of our emotions, yet without sinning. As a result of His having gone through the total human experience, Christ is the
ultimate encourager, not only in times of grief and crisis but
at all times and in all things.

THINGS *NOT* TO SAY OR DO

There are some things I suggest that you *not* say to a grieving person.

First, if children are left behind, never hint to them
that their mother, father, brother, sister, or grandparent
was called by God "because He needed a good mother"
(or other statement of relationship). The fact is, God
does not *need* us. We need God. Furthermore, if a child
thinks that God took his mother or father because He
"needed" her or him, what kind of image will that child
have of God? How could the child possibly grow in his
love for a God he cannot see who took his parent whom
he loved and held and depended on every day? A child is
likely to respond in the depth of his young spirit, "I
needed this person even more than God does!" A child
may easily become frightened and angry at this line of
thinking, too, because the next logical step is to think
that God may "need" him also.

Second, do *not* ask for details related to the death of the
loved one. In the very early stages of my grief, I wished
many times that people had not asked for details related to
either Suzan's illness or death. At the time those facts were
too painful for me. However, the Redhead didn't mind
answering questions at all.

Third, there are those who say and believe that Satan
killed or snatched away the loved one. Scripturally that is

inaccurate. Again Psalm 139:16 asserts that God, not Satan, has our days numbered. Christ met Satan in battle and defeated him. Satan is a created being, and the creation is no match for the Creator. Romans 8:38–39 assures us that *nothing* can separate us from the love of God that is in Christ Jesus our Lord.

WHAT ABOUT NONBELIEVERS?

What about the person who loses someone precious to him but has no certainty that the loved one is secure in the arms of Christ or that the person will enjoy a blessed eternity with Him? What can we say to give that grieving person encouragement?

I do not believe in false hope, and I do not claim to understand everything about God, but I do understand His awesome love. I know that hell was created for the fallen angels and that a merciful God has given man a specific means of escaping hell and that escape is linked to choice. The one hope I believe all of us can cling to is that deep down inside, everyone—even the most renowned atheist—believes there really is a God. On what basis do I make this statement? Let me give you several reasons.

For a number of years, Brown Trucking in Atlanta, Georgia, gave a lie detector test to every person hired (until it became illegal to do so). The company had more than a hundred terminals throughout the United States. A series of questions was asked during this polygraph test. After the test was well under way, one of the questions was, "Do you believe there is a God?" In literally thousands of cases, every time an individual said no, the needle on the polygraph went berserk, indicating that he was lying, that deep down inside the person really did believe there was a God.

Some time ago, three Christian missionaries were murdered by natives in the jungles of South America. Several years later their wives went into the same area and led the chiefs of those tribes to a saving knowledge of Christ. The change in their lives was so dramatic and their lives were so completely enriched by their newfound faith that two of the chiefs eventually traveled to the United States and gave their testimonies in a number of churches. The chiefs said that during the time before their acceptance of Christ, they knew there was "a God up there" who was not pleased that they were killing people. Those men, however, had never heard of Christ or what it meant to be a Christian. Even so, God revealed Himself to them in the heavens as well as in nature.

The Bible tells us that God will judge us based on the amount of our information and knowledge. The one who is brought up in a Christian home and who has attended church every Sunday for years will have a considerable amount of knowledge, regardless of how little attention he might have been paying. God will deal with that person differently from the way He will deal with the person who has never heard the gospel, such as those people of the jungle. However, the people must respond to the knowledge they have before God will reveal the "rest of the story."

The thief who hung on the cross next to Jesus is yet another reason I have hope on behalf of the departed loved one. At the last instant, it seems, he recognized Christ for who He was, was forgiven, and is now spending eternity with Christ. Those who face imminent death may confess that Jesus is Lord and believe in their hearts that God raised Jesus from death, even if no other person knows they have done so. According to the Scriptures, those who confess Christ in this way *will* enter the kingdom. I readily admit that this is not nearly as comforting as the comfort known by those whose departed loved one was deeply committed to Christ and had grown in Christ's grace and love. Still, heaven doesn't really have any back-row seats, although there are different rewards for believers who enter heaven.

By no stretch of the imagination should this encourage a person to become slack in commitment and service to the Lord. To think that a person can plan to have opportunity for a deathbed or last-second commitment to Christ is foolishness. Heaven is too sweet, and hell is too hot, to gamble with salvation, especially when God has given us a clear and certain way of securing our eternal future. The instructions on how to receive God's offer of free salvation are sprinkled throughout His Book. I encourage you to read prayerfully every instance related to one's salvation and eternal life.

IN CASES OF SUICIDE

At 7:30 A.M., Thursday, January 12, 1997, I received one of the most shocking and heartbreaking phone calls I have ever received. Larry and Lisa Carpenter, whom I regard almost as my children because I have known them so well for so many years, called to tell me that Larry's brother, Danny, had taken his own life. Lisa was the one who made the call, and she told me that Larry was not handling the situation well, which was completely understandable. Larry had been more than a big brother to Danny. In many ways, he was like a father or mentor to Danny. They were extremely close. Larry had felt a strong responsibility for Danny and obviously loved him very much. My conversation with Larry was difficult because I began weeping and could not stop. Larry and I did manage to communicate a few thoughts, and Larry, at least for the moment, seemed to feel a little better by our conversation's end.

There is no way any of us can know exactly how Larry felt in that moment and how his parents felt, because no one else knows the depth of love between any two people. What we can understand more clearly perhaps are the many questions that arise in these situations. Was there anything I could have done? Why didn't Danny call for help? What was wrong? These questions are not limited to cases of suicide, but also apply to deaths related to illnesses or accidents.

As best I could, I assured Larry that God knew before Danny was even conceived that his days were numbered. God knew exactly on which day Danny would go home. I told Larry what he already knew—namely, that Danny was committed to Christ and he was safely in His arms and would experience no more pain. I tried to assure Larry that there was nothing any of us could have done, and I told Larry that one of the beauties of knowing Christ is the fact that we are not called to feel a sense of guilt for the actions of another person. When we have loved and have done the best we knew to do and were able to do, that's all God requires of us. Furthermore, God would not trust one of His own—and Danny was His own—either to the mistakes or to the neglect of other people, including a much-loved brother, father, mother, or sister.

Larry and I talked about Romans 8:28 (NKJV) that clearly states, "All things work together for good to those who love God, to those who are the called according to His purpose." I reminded Larry that this verse does not say that every *one* thing is for our good, but that *all* things, under

the direction of a loving God, *working together,* are good.
There is no good in the act of suicide itself. As the pastor at
Danny's services so beautifully pointed out, what Danny did
was wrong. He put himself in God's hands and then made
his own decision to take his own life. It was wrong that he
did not confide how badly he was hurting to his family, his
pastor, his physician, or countless numbers of people who
loved him. Nevertheless, *God* is the One who works *all things*
together for good.

Danny had been a police officer for seven years, was
extremely popular, and had a host of friends—evidenced in
part by the tremendous overflow of people in the church
for the funeral services. With a bright career in front of
him, a wife beside him, and a beautiful baby daughter
depending on him, *why* would Danny take his life? The
question of why is often asked about the death of a person,
perhaps especially so in cases of suicide.

According to his family, Danny had been suffering from
excruciating headaches and had been at least mildly
depressed. Yet, no one had any idea that he was that
depressed or in that much pain. The conclusion must be
reached, as it always must be reached: *only God knows the full
answer to the* why *questions.*

One thing we can always count on in the death of a
believer in Christ is that while God may not approve of
every action we take—including the act of suicide—the
blood of Christ was spilled on Calvary, and it provides forgiveness for all our sins, regardless of what they may be.

Some people have asked me whether I believe that a
person who takes his own life can still go to heaven. My
answer is an emphatic *yes.* Some argue, "But he had no
chance for forgiveness." That may be true—for the case of
this one sin. But let me point out that unless we all die as we

are praying for forgiveness of our sins, we *all* are likely to die with unforgiven and unrepented sin of some type. Furthermore, Danny had accepted the forgiveness of Christ and had committed his life to Christ. Christ's blood was shed for *all* the sins Danny had committed and would ever commit. When Christ died, roughly two thousand years before Danny's appearance on this earth, He died for *all* of Danny's sins. Danny was born with the sins Christ knew he was going to commit already forgiven. The only requirement Danny had to meet for eternal life was to receive Christ's forgiveness and commit his life to following Christ, something he had done many years ago.

Not long after Danny died—on February 2, 1997—I talked again with Larry and Lisa, mostly with Larry. He was doing much better, but obviously was still grieving. Larry pointed out that he had been overwhelmed with gratitude at the large number of friends who had stopped by, called, or dropped him a note, assuring him of their prayers and support. He had been comforted at knowing a host of people genuinely cared for him and were concerned about his family.

Toward the close of our conversation, Larry told me about something that had happened as he and his six-and-a-half-year-old son, Alex, were walking one day. Larry was quietly grieving, tears streaming down his cheeks, when little Alex put his hand in Larry's and said, "Dad, Danny is okay. He's with Jesus." Then Alex said something that only God could have inspired. He said, "Dad, I've been talking to Jesus for longer than I can remember, and He told me that we are not to worry about Danny. He is with Jesus now and everything is going to be okay."

You have to reflect only a few moments to know that a six-and-a-half-year-old does not have that kind of wisdom and insight as the result of human teaching. God was clearly speaking through the child to comfort Larry's heart. I am convinced that God was able to speak through Alex because Larry and Lisa taught Alex about the love of Christ from the time they got up until the time they went to bed, whether they were at the dinner table or on walks, whether they were tucking their children into bed or taking them to church. All of those deposits of faith they had made into Alex's mind, as well as into the mind of Alex's twin brother, had prepared Alex to be used by the Lord in just that moment in just that way. It is truly marvelous to know that whatever battle we are in, we have already won—not because of what we do or have done, but because of what Christ did and continues to do.

Ultimately the Lord knows precisely the words that *He* desires for you to speak to comfort another person. Ask Him to speak through you to that person who needs to hear a God-inspired word. Ask Him to reveal to you what you might write in a letter or card. Ask Him if there is a particular book, booklet, or piece of music that would be appropriate for you to share. Ask Him when you might go to that person to be "present" for him, possibly to have lunch or go on a walk, so that you might listen, share the sorrow, and perhaps give a hug.

The Lord who allows each of us to grieve differently also knows and provides precisely what will bring comfort to our hearts.

13

GIVING TO OTHERS
OUT OF
YOUR GRIEF

No matter who we are, and no matter how we are feeling or what we are going through, God can still use us to minister His love and care to another person. That is a wonderful and awesome mystery of God. He chooses to use us to help others and, in the process, bring greater healing to ourselves.

One day while I was walking, I reflected on my mother, who lost her baby and her husband in less than a week. At the time, we were living out in the country where my father was the overseer for a large farm. I can only imagine her grief, mingled with fear and concern for her family. How would she manage to support and raise eleven children without him? Surely that must have been a time so difficult that very few people who read this book can comprehend it.

Later, my mother lost two of her sons. They were adults by then, but one of them was only forty-two years old when he died suddenly of a heart attack. I loved my brother, but at that point, I could not comprehend what my mother might be going through in her grief. She lost a second son to emphysema. He died in his early fifties, and I watched him suffer for months in the hospital. As painful as his death was, we all had some time to prepare for it. My mother's grief, compounded by all the other factors of her difficult life, must have been nearly unbearable.

As I thought about my mother's experience, I came to the realization that no matter how intensely we may hurt in our grief, there is very likely someone with whom we would never want to trade places. There is always someone who seems to have a worse situation than the one we face.

Although it is difficult for me to imagine anyone losing someone more dear to him than Suzan was to me, the suddenness of loss, the tragedy of circumstances, or the loss of more than one family member can create a situation in which I say, "I am glad I didn't have to experience that." I am grateful that I had the opportunity to repeatedly reassure my daughter of my love for her, and I am grateful that others in our family had those same opportunities. I am grateful that I had my daughter with me as long as I did. I am grateful for the life she lived. As deep as the pain of her death is to me, I also have many reasons to say, "I am thankful."

Ike Reighard, for example, is someone with whom I wouldn't have wanted to trade places. He lost both his wife and unborn baby in a tragic turn of events. He literally was walking down the hallway toward the waiting room, expecting at any moment to receive the joyful news that his wife had given birth to their child, when he received instead the shattering news that both of them had died. I can hardly imagine the pain he must have felt in that moment.

Nor can I imagine the grief that a parent must feel if a

child is lost in an automobile wreck, a drive-by shooting, or any type of accident. I am grateful that there was no one else involved in Suzan's death—that she wasn't the victim of a car jacking or in an accident involving a drunken driver.

I am grateful that Suzan's death didn't come without any warning. We had fifteen days in the hospital with her to adjust to the fact that she was dying and to repeatedly express our love to her. During that period, she was on life support for nearly nine days, so she could not respond to our questions with anything other than a nod of her head. Even so, we could communicate our love to her, pray with her, give her as much hope and encouragement as we could, and comfort her with our presence. In many ways, we had a chance to prepare for what eventually became the reality that we had to face. We also had the opportunity to weep and be comforted by others in the family. I am grateful to the Lord for that time, especially for the last week, which seemed like a bonus week to us.

ONLY WHAT WE CAN BEAR

Never have I been as sure as I am in the aftermath of Suzan's death that God gives us only what we are able to bear.

As difficult as it is for me to comprehend losing a child in a sudden accident, I am aware that parents in such situations also seem to experience a special grace of God to do so.

After she had attended a seminar where I spoke, Rebecca Greer of London, Kentucky, sent me one of the most heartbreaking notes I have ever received. She wrote,

"I came [to the seminar] to get motivation to live—just living is a struggle for me." Rebecca added that sixteen years earlier, she and her husband, Gam, had lost their two-year-old son, Stephen, to leukemia, and then on January 16, 1995, an almost unspeakable tragedy took the lives of Buzzy, Todd, and Kami, their other three children.

At the time of the more recent tragedy, the Greers appeared to be an all-American family. Gam was a successful businessman, active in the community, participating fully in his children's lives, attending their extracurricular activities, coaching basketball, soccer, and softball, and attending church with them. Rebecca worked a few hours a week at a Christian bookstore, but her relationship with God and her family responsibilities were her first priorities.

The only apparent cloud on the Greer family horizon was an involvement with drugs by their twenty-three-year-old son, Buzzy. He was living at home after an arrest for possession of marijuana, and he was to enter a drug rehabilitation program on January 17. The events of January 16, however, totally destroyed those plans.

The family was having dinner when Buzzy received a phone call from a woman he had been dating for a couple of months. She called to tell him their relationship was over. Buzzy, unbeknownst to his parents, had purchased a gun, and roughly two minutes after the phone call, he stood up at the dinner table and began shooting at his family members. Gam believes in retrospect that the call, combined with Buzzy's withdrawal from drugs, caused him to snap. Gam and Rebecca are both quick to note that while Buzzy's actions might indicate that he did not love his family, they believe the exact opposite was true. He had always dearly loved his brother and sister, as well as his parents, but drugs had taken an unfathomable toll on him.

Sister Kami and brother Todd were killed. Gam was wounded, but managed to escape to the basement and dial 911, even though he couldn't see the numbers. Rebecca was trying to phone for help in the kitchen when Buzzy forced her into the basement. When Buzzy looked away for a moment, Rebecca escaped and ran toward a neighbor's house. Buzzy followed, firing shots at her. Then he made a dash for the family car.

The police chased Buzzy through the south end of town, and eventually he crashed through a police blockade, lost control of the car, and slid into a ditch. There, in the car, he put his .380 pistol to his head and fired the gun one last time.

With Rebecca's permission, I share the rest of the note she wrote to us:

> I became a Christian as a child but after losing my first child, my faith became *very* strong and I had a close relationship with God. I tried to live my life as He wanted me to, and raised my children to love Him.
>
> Since my recent tragedy, however, I am lost. I can't find hope or purpose or meaning in my life. I have lost God—or He has lost me. Do you have a word of hope for me, or do you know someone who does? I feel I'm at a place [level of understanding] that very few people have been and I can't find anyone to relate to.
>
> Do you know of any books, tapes, articles—ANYTHING that can help me?

Rebecca's note spoke volumes to me about the depth of her grief. I wrote her and sent her a copy of Dr. James Dobson's book, *When God Doesn't Make Sense.* I let her know that I easily understood why she had such negative feelings about faith and hope, but I also pointed out to her the words of the apostle Peter, who concluded that in the face of reality's harshest moments, "Where else can we turn?" God is truly the one and only Answer to life, even with all of its mysteries, and eventually we find our way back to Him.

After I received that first note from Rebecca, I developed a friendship with her and Gam through the sharing of our grief. I have shared with them in correspondence some of what is in this book. In May of 1996, I received a letter from Rebecca, which she has also given me permission to share:

> I am pleased to tell you that I am finding my way back to God and I want you to know that you played a part in that and I am very grateful. I still have dark times, but not *as dark* and not for as long of periods.
>
> My husband and I are in counseling with a very fine Christian man. He has been very helpful. I am back in church again, though still not as involved as I once was. The sermon last week was on the dangers of drugs and alcohol and our pastor asked me to speak. It was very difficult for me. (I am not a gifted speaker.) Maybe you could give me some pointers! I was able to share with the young people of our church about my son Buzzy. I told them that he was a "regular kid" just like they are, but that he made wrong choices that affected a lot of people in very painful ways. Even though it is very hard for me to speak in front of people, I find that each time I do, there is some healing for me. People continue to ask me to speak to young people and my initial response is "NO WAY! I can't do that." I end up telling myself that if it will help just one child, it will be worth it for me to be uncomfortable for a while. Please pray for me that I will become more comfortable speaking in

front of people so that I can share our story with the
hope that it will help someone.

Considering the magnitude of her loss, Rebecca has
made and continues to make considerable progress in dealing with her grief. As I neared completion of this book, I
wrote and asked for her input on specific ways she and Gam
dealt with their loss and grief. Here is her response:

> We have just come through a particularly difficult time
> and are looking forward to spring. The holidays are
> very difficult for us and the anniversary date of our
> tragedy is January 16. So, the winter months can seem
> very, very long. We bought a second home in Hilton
> Head, South Carolina, so that we would have a place to
> go to when things get "too heavy" at home. It has been
> a lifesaver, especially for me. I was a stay-at-home mom
> so there are many, many more memories and reminders
> for me at home than for Gam. At times it can be
> overwhelming and I just need to get away. Many people
> sell their homes and start out somewhere else, but in
> our case, Gam actually draws strength from our home
> and does not want to live anywhere else. That is how we
> came to a "compromise" of a second home. I guess I
> have gone the long way around to say that we have
> learned something very important that has helped us
> survive as a couple. We recognize and appreciate that
> everyone grieves differently.
>
> Prayer, of course, has been very important in helping
> us deal with our pain and grief. Even during the dark
> times when we do not have the energy to pray we know
> that others (many that we don't even know) are lifting
> us up in prayer. Just yesterday a woman that I've never

heard of called me to thank me for writing my article on my spiritual crisis and she shared with me that she remembers us in prayer every day. Where would any of us be without prayer?

Being outside in nature has been very helpful to me in my grief process. I draw strength being outside in God's beautiful creation.

Talking about your feelings and your experience is very important. It can be difficult to find someone who is willing to listen to you say the same things over and over. It is also difficult to find someone who is willing to hear your pain. People want to avoid pain. Gam and I were able to find a pastoral counselor that we connected with and we have been seeing him for three years.

Ideally, it would be wonderful if everyone had friends or family who would be willing to listen, but in the fast-paced lifestyle that we live in, it seems that people who have that kind of time, or who are willing to give that kind of time, are few and far between. I do believe that listening or just "being there" is the most important thing people can do for loved ones who are hurting. It can mean so much more than bringing over a casserole. So much more . . .

People who have reached out to me have played a very big role in helping me through my struggle. As I have told you before, Zig, your letters and phone calls meant so much to me. One thing I specifically remember you sharing with me was that I should let my friends help me—that it would be giving them a "gift" to let them do something for us. Thank you for reaching out to me and helping me find my way out of a very dark time. If all of us would just reach out to one another in love as God calls us to do, what a better world this would be.

Reading books or articles on grief has been helpful to me. When I read about or hear stories of other people who have survived tragedies it helps me to realize that I am not alone and it gives me hope that I can survive as well.

Other things that Gam and I have done to help us deal with our pain and loss is to try to keep the memory of our children alive. We started a "Greer Children Memorial Fund" at our church, which will go toward a new Christian Life Center. We have given a "Greer Children Memorial Scholarship" to a senior boy and a senior girl for the past three years. I have spoken to several schools and church groups about how drugs can destroy lives—and whenever I speak, I consider that I speak in memory of my children.

There are three major points I would like to emphasize about the Greers. First, the Greers are making progress—serious progress—in dealing with their grief, though they have not gotten over it, simply because no one ever gets over it. They are working through their grief, and with God's grace and love, they will not only survive and make it in life, but they will be a marvelous example to others who are experiencing deep grief.

The second point is the one I shared in an earlier chapter—we grieve in different ways. Rebecca and her husband, though they had shared the same roof for many years, are dealing with the loss of their family members in different ways. The message is that no one can instruct or teach others exactly how to deal with their grief. Thoughts, ideas, and suggestions can be offered, but only the one who is suffering the grief will know which way works best for him.

The third point is this: in the midst of Rebecca's grief, she is giving to others. God is using her to help others, and in the process, He is bringing about greater strength and wholeness in her.

I believe God gives such opportunities to every person who is grieving. Look around you. Who *needs* you, even though you feel shattered, weakened, and in the deep pain of sorrow? That could be the very person God desires for you to help in ways that only you can.

SENSITIVITY TO PEOPLE WHO GRIEVE ALONGSIDE YOU

Some of the people to whom God may desire for you to give are likely to be those who are closest to you and to your departed loved one. Although the grieving process may be highly individualized, much about grieving can be shared with another person who is grieving about the same loss.

Throughout our grieving experience, our daughters, Cindy and Julie, and our son, Tom, have expressed intense concern for their mother and me. All of them are hurting terribly in their great love and respect for their sister, yet they have sensed the depth of their parents' sorrow and their love for us has motivated them to be equally sensitive to our pain. What a wonderful privilege it is to have such precious children who seek to minister to others, even through their tears and sorrow! I do not know how I would have handled the overwhelming personal grief I felt at Suzan's homegoing if it had not been for the incredible support, love, and affection shown to me by my wife and our three other children, as well as their spouses.

As much as I loved Suzan and do not believe that any one person could have loved her more, and as much as I miss her, I recognize that the Redhead misses Suzan even more than I do. Suzan was her best friend. They had lunch together once or twice a week, and when I was on the road, the Redhead was frequently invited to have dinner with Suzan and her family. They often dropped in on each other, and almost every day they were on the telephone from one to three times, sometimes talking up to an hour or more. They thoroughly enjoyed each other's company. At least a couple of times a week they would do something special together, such as take Elizabeth to a movie or go shopping. They could shop for a half day and not buy anything! Being together was what mattered.

For the Redhead, the loss of Suzan creates a gaping hole in her daily routine.

BE AWARE OF THE NEEDS OF OTHERS

During the Christmas and New Year's season following Suzan's death, I had occasion to reflect on the grief our family was experiencing, and I realized that the grief and sadness that many of us in the family had felt had not occurred for each one of us in the same ways or with the same intensity.

Over the holidays the Redhead and I took a short trip out to the cemetery where Suzan is buried. It was the first time we had been there since Suzan's grave marker had been put in place, so it was a grief-filled time for both of us. Looking at her grave marker, I wondered about the varying intensity of grief that each member of our family has felt.

Grief does not rest entirely on the amount of love we had for the deceased. In some cases, grief seems intensified based upon the *need* a person had for the loved one. The need that Chad felt for his wife and Katherine felt for her mother was greater than my need for Suzan as a daughter and coworker, and although I doubt that either could have loved Suzan more than I did, the need they had for her in their lives compounded their grief.

In Chad's case, Suzan had been his mate for seventeen years, and almost without exception she was the first person he saw in the morning and the last person he saw at night. Even in the final days of her life, when she was having difficulty breathing and had to use oxygen while she slept, she and Chad continued to sleep in the same bed, although both might have been more comfortable with another sleeping arrangement. Suzan, I believe, sensed the end was near, and she did not want to lose one precious moment of being close to Chad. She continued to take care of everything around the house—she paid the bills, bought and prepared food, talked with Katherine, and did all of the things a committed wife and mother does. At her death, Chad suddenly had to take on all of these daily responsibilities. His need for her was great, his missing her has been intense, and his love for her was immense.

Katherine also misses her mother in a very significant way. Suzan talked with Katherine virtually every moment she could. She guided her and shared with her in making the daily decisions Katherine faced. Chad was more the role model because his work schedule did not allow for the same number of hours in a day that Suzan shared with Katherine. Suzan was more the hands-on teacher. She was also the major communicator in her family. Katherine's need for her mother was and is intense, and her need has compounded her grief.

Recognizing the depth of need and grief in another person is not the same, of course, as doing something to meet that need or speak comfort to the grief.

Let me give you just one small example of how the Redhead and our daughter Cindy acted to help meet a need in Katherine's life.

One day while the Redhead was talking to Cindy—a frequent and ordinary occurrence—the Redhead suggested that Cindy might need some "Katherine time." Cindy laughed and happily said, "I agree! Let's all get together."

The three of them met at a movie theater, and as they were watching the movie, Katherine leaned her head on Cindy's shoulder. She then put her leg across Cindy's, as she had done so many times with Suzan. Suddenly she realized what she was doing, and she apologized, saying, "Aunt Cindy, I shouldn't do this." Cindy replied, "Oh, yes, you should, Katherine. I love it, and you know, I don't have any children. You're the closest thing to a daughter I'll ever have, so keep it up, Katherine!"

Cindy was there for Katherine in a way that was comfortable and meaningful *to* Katherine and, in many ways, also comfortable and meaningful to Cindy. How grateful I am for family members who are willing to show love to one another.

At times it is easy to become self-centered in our grief and to think that nobody hurts as badly as we hurt or that nobody loved as much as we loved. That very rarely is the case, and even if it is the case, such a self-focused approach is never beneficial to a person's healing from grief. We are wise to turn our eyes outward, to see the needs of others around us, and to reach out to them as best we can. In that, we will find blessing and healing.

A WILLINGNESS TO SHARE GRIEF

Although most of this chapter has dealt with our *giving* to others out of our grief, there is also an important lesson for us to learn in being able to *share* our grief with others and to actively receive what they desire to give us.

When someone offers you an expression of comfort or care, don't turn it away! Receive it. Embrace it. Let that person give to you, and actively choose to take into your heart the love and care that he desires to give. Not only will you be enriched by his expression of love, but he will be made stronger for having made the expression.

In the process of my grieving I have realized that words of comfort and shared grief from my "old" friends have been meaningful to me in a way that is different from the expressions of comfort and shared grief from newer friends or the friends of Suzan. That does not mean that I value any more or less any expression of comfort extended to me. All have been helpful. It is to say that expressions from childhood friends or long-standing friends have had a different quality to them.

About a month after Suzan died, I received a call from Earl Small, a friend from the early days of my marriage. He had just received word that Suzan had died. I had been instrumental in Earl's leaving his paper mill job and going on to outstanding success, first as a salesperson, then as a sales manager, and finally as the national manager of a major direct sales company. We had watched each other's children grow up, marry, and have children of their own. It was comforting to know that an old friend shared my heartbreak.

In the 1970s I worked for several years with Dan Bellus, an extremely articulate, very compassionate, bright man, perhaps the most knowledgeable man in the country in regard to time management. He was also a real people person. During our years together, he developed a friendship with Suzan. They became soul mates and Dan served as friend, counselor, and encourager, helping her through some difficult times in her life. Over a period of time, Dan and I lost contact and rarely saw or talked to each other. As a result, I did not realize just how much he and Suzan meant to each other, so I did not let Dan know of her illness and death.

On Wednesday, May 24, I received a call from Dan. He had just gotten the news of Suzan's death and was absolutely crushed. It seems that over the years he and Suzan had periodically visited on the telephone. Suzan loved and respected Dan very much. In my telephone conversation with him, a heartbroken Dan told me that he loved Suzan more than anybody on earth, outside his own immediate family.

He said, "She was as much like a daughter to me as my own Barbara, and we had a bond that few people of different generations have. There was something very special about Suzan and something very, very special about our relationship. I was *crushed* when I heard of Suzan's death. I was so proud of her accomplishment in achieving a happy and comfortable life, and it was so heartbreaking to see it end so prematurely." His praise of her was beautiful, and his broken heart came through in unmistakable tones. When I offered to send him a recording of the funeral service, he responded with gratitude. I was touched by all that Dan shared with me.

Shared grief builds and deepens a relationship. And over time, a deep relationship gives freedom to share grief. The process is cyclical.

Certainly the one person who can most thoroughly share my grief is the Redhead. One morning she found me weeping. Her first words were, "You miss her, don't you?" We embraced, and as we did, I thought how marvelous it is to have someone to share my grief, someone who genuinely loves me and who loved the same daughter. Many times the Redhead knows how I am feeling and what I am thinking about Suzan without a word being spoken. She truly shares my grief. To me, the Redhead has been a five-foot-one-inch tower of pure faith, love, strength, courage, and encouragement.

I cannot tell you how important it has been to me to have the most important person in my life close to me as I grieve. What a blessing it has been to have a lifetime relationship with someone who really knew and loved Suzan just as much as I did. I encourage you to develop a relationship with your spouse that is such that you can share how you feel at all times, openly and lovingly. When times of grief arise, a spouse who has deeply shared your life will be the most valuable friend you can have.

LOOK FOR GOD-GIVEN OPPORTUNITIES TO GIVE

Be alert to all of the opportunities God will give you to share the grief of another person. Keep in mind that this person may be the one who is closest to you! Look for the ways God may lead you to give to another who is also grieving.

As we give, we receive. And in that giving and receiving process, God heals our hearts.

14

KEEPING
THE RELATIONSHIP
ALIVE

O<small>N WHAT WOULD</small> have been Suzan's forty-eighth birthday, I visited her grave and asked myself, If I had a choice of Suzan remaining in heaven or returning to life on earth, what would I choose? My answer, as you might have guessed, would be that under no circumstances would I ask her to leave the perfection of heaven.

On the other hand, I can readily imagine what it would be like if suddenly Suzan were here with me for a few minutes. I would instantly grab her, hug her, and weep. Then, knowing what a great sense of humor she had, I would probably say, "Suzan, what on earth did you do that caused God to kick you out of your mansion on a street paved with gold, where all you had to do was praise and worship Him? What did you do, Doll, to be sent back *here*, even for a moment?"

Suzan frequently reminded her mother and me, as well as her sisters and brother, that she was the "favorite child." She did this in a teasing way, and we all understood she was teasing. She often started phone conversations with her mother by saying, "This is your favorite child." I can imagine that Suzan would laugh at my question and reply, "Well, you know, Dad, I'll have to confess that I wasn't the favorite in heaven where God had all those great prophets close to Him. Although I did rate pretty close to the top, I thought I'd come back here for a moment where I am *the* favorite. God also thought it would be neat if I came back and told you what a wonderful place heaven is and how marvelous it is not to have any pain or problems. So, Dad, knowing that you and Mom and the rest of the family still have to deal with problems, I want to encourage you to keep the faith and to know that we'll all be in heaven together one day."

An imaginary conversation like that with Suzan brings me joy, not pain.

One acronym for GRIEF is God's Relief in Eternal Fellowship. I find it very helpful to see grief from this perspective. My fellowship with Suzan has not ended because she is in heaven. She is still very much present in my mind and heart.

It is easy for me to imagine Suzan saying a number of things to us, including things she would say to us if she saw us crying in sadness or feeling the deep inner pain of grief. She would likely tease us a little about our many tears, she would encourage us to quit crying and start laughing, and she might even invite us to come on home with her!

How do I know this? Because I know Suzan! I have forty-six years of experience in knowing her and in enjoying her personality. I know how she would respond to many situations, what she would like and dislike, and about what she would express approval or disapproval. Her opinions and ideas and feelings have always been important to me, and they continue to be important.

CONVERSING WITH YOUR
DEPARTED LOVED ONE

Based on my personal experience as well as fairly extensive reading and conversations that I have had with a number of other people who have lost loved ones, I believe that one of the healthiest ways to deal with the loss is to engage in a loving conversation with the person who has died.

Now I am not talking about a séance or about any pretense at an actual conversation with the departed person. Engaging in that type of activity is described as a blatant violation of God's commandments. Rather, I am talking about a willingness to continue to think about and to talk to the person who has died as if he is still with you. I believe it is a serious mistake to try to forget the person or to deny the intricate and extensive ways that person has been a part of your thinking and conversing for years or decades.

My wife and I have mentioned many times that we were privileged to teach Suzan how to live, but she had a far greater privilege—that of teaching us how to die. Suzan, in her death, had an impact on me that has been indescribable. As we watched her in those last days, and as we talked with her and observed her faith, she taught us by her example what it means to die in Christ. As we have heard friend after friend, person after person, and family members tell us their own favorite "Suzie stories," we have been encouraged and have realized anew the impact she had on many, many lives. We are grateful she was our daughter so that we might experience her life.

These are things that I tell Suzie in my mind and heart. I tell her how grateful I am for the lessons she taught me. I tell her how grateful I am for the witness of Christ she gave to family members and close friends and casual acquaintances.

COUNTING IN HER OPINION

I recall one joyful day about six months after Suzan's death. I had risen earlier than usual and had been able to spend about an hour studying my Bible. Then I enjoyed a leisurely breakfast with the Redhead before I joined my son at the golf course. I played exceptionally well—my score of 79 was the best I have ever had on that particular course, considered to be one of the toughest in the Dallas area. As much fun as I had playing golf with my son, who incidentally shot a 73, I had even more fun at lunch. We were joined by the Redhead and our two daughters Julie and Cindy. Everyone was in a great mood as we went back and forth through the buffet line at the club. We were laughing and talking and expressing gratitude to our Lord for His goodness to us.

Through it all, I found myself thinking, *Suzan would have been having a ball.* I had no trouble imagining that if Suzan had been present, she would have taken the seat at the end of the table and designated it "the seat of honor," which she routinely did as part of establishing her position as the "favorite child." Everyone would have gone along with Suzan's actions because everyone in the family knew that the Redhead and I love each of our children equally and we have never had favorites.

A little more than two months after Suzan died, the Redhead and I went to Sugarville, our Holly Lake home, for four days of relaxation. One of my terms of affection for my wife is Sugar Baby, so it is only natural that our lake house would have a sugar-related name. We have spent many pleasurable times there as a family. Certainly July 21, 1995, was just such a day. Cindy came out to the lake with her dog, Emmitt. We recalled, of course, that Sugarville was one of Suzan's favorite places. The quiet and peaceful atmosphere there gave her considerable pleasure.

Our daughter Cindy is a great one for bringing some of these memories back and for noting, "Suz would have loved this!" On that particular day, Cindy and I recalled that Suz always loved going to Petty's, our family's favorite "country cafe" where a person can get seventy-five grams of fat, four thousand calories, and an overloaded stomach for $5.95. Cindy also noted that the beautiful new restaurant at the lake, which serves delicious food of a less-fattening nature, was one that deserved the praise, "Suz would have loved this!" The truth is, Suzan loved a lot of things and a lot of people.

FREEDOM TO TALK ABOUT
YOUR LOVED ONE

Talking freely with my family and friends about Suzan's death has been helpful to me in working through my grief. My children, and especially my wife and daughters—perhaps because women are more inclined to show their emotions and verbalize their feelings—often talk about Suzan when they are together.

The last week in 1997, the Redhead and I spent several days at our Holly Lake home with Cindy and Richard. Tom and Chachis, along with little Alexandra, joined us for a day. It was a happy occasion, but as always, on my walks with Cindy, we spent part of our time talking about Suzan. It is natural to talk about someone you love. That is true whether the person is alive on this earth or present with the Lord. *Not* to talk about Suzan would be unnatural to both Cindy and me.

I believe that conversation is a priceless healer.

It's strange, isn't it, that we tend to think a broken heart should be dealt with in a totally different way from a broken arm or leg. We know that a broken bone needs attention. So does a broken heart. The healing process for a broken bone is clear-cut, simple, and fairly short. There is nothing clear-cut or simple—and the duration certainly is not short—for healing a broken heart. Nevertheless, talking is great broken-heart therapy, and remember, the line to Jesus Christ is always open!

ACKNOWLEDGING THE ONGOING INFLUENCE

Going through some of my files several months after Suzan died, I came across a note from her about a column we had been working on. Her note was short, but the suggestion that she had made, and that I had followed, was insightful and good. She had a wonderful way of boldly giving me information and insight and yet, at the same time, expressing her ideas in a loving manner that was very respectful and that made me *want* to take her advice. As always, she had signed the note, "YFC, Suzie." (YFC stands for Your Favorite Child.)

As I reflected on Suzan's note, I realized that Suzan has influenced not only my life as a father, but also my work as a writer. She has made me more aware of the way in which I might effectively and more lovingly express my ideas. I am grateful for that.

A few weeks after Suzan died, I found a note in my office

from Laurie Magers, my executive assistant, that said, "If you haven't already noticed it, look on your Wall of Gratitude." This wall contains pictures of men and women who have had a significant impact on my life. A new photo had been added to the wall, bringing the total number of photos to twenty-one. It was a photo of Suzan, which Chad had graciously enlarged. Seeing her picture there, I realized anew that Suzan truly has had a dramatic impact on my life and influenced me in my day-to-day activities. I dearly loved to talk with her. She was bright and sensitive and had a loving nature. I admired her extensive vocabulary and her sensitivity in seeking just the right words to convey the best ideas and feelings.

On a walk one day I imagined what Suzan would say to me if she were able to write me a letter. Here's what I thought she might say:

Dear Dad:

In your lifetime you have been excited about a lot of things, and one of your delights in life has been to play golf. I always wished you would take more time to play, but I knew you had other priorities and things you felt you had to do—plus all the things you *wanted* to do with us girls, Mom, and Tom. I just want you to know, Dad, that I watched you a couple of weeks ago when you were playing Muirfield, which was one of those courses you had on your list of "things to do and courses to play." I'm sorry the weather was not perfect, and I regret that you were not playing better than you were. I could not help noticing, however, that you did hit a few good tee shots and that you sank a couple of nice long putts, and it was exciting to see that you've lost none of your exuberance or enthusiasm for the game of golf. I know you

have an exuberance about a lot of things, and I know
you are especially excited about heaven.

Well, Dad, I've got to tell you, I don't believe you
have a clue about what is in store for you. You have a
pretty good imagination, but there's nothing like
heaven, Dad. You know that the Bible says, "Eye has not
seen and ear has not heard about the real glories of
God," but I'm here to tell you, Dad, that those words
are *true*! I can't tell you everything, Dad, because I
promised the Lord I wouldn't. We have to keep some
secrets, you know, and we can't let you see all the way to
the other side. But, Dad, if there were golf courses in
heaven—and I'm not going to say whether there are or
are not—I'm just here to tell you that they would make
Augusta National look like a small-town, unkempt
municipal course that has no greenkeeper or superin-
tendent to look after the fairways.

Up here, Dad, if there *were* golf courses, they would
be so incredibly beautiful that you just might not be
able to take your eyes off the beauty and concentrate on
hitting the ball. Oh, I've heard you say a lot of times
that you've got to "keep your eyes on the ball; keep your
head still; slow, smooth backswing; don't try to kill it,
just be composed." Well, up here, Dad, you would get so
carried away with just looking at the course, I'm not certain if you'd ever get around to hitting the ball! But if
you did, Dad, those 300-yard drives that you only dream
about now would most certainly be a reality, and hitting
those fairway woods 250 yards to the green would be
commonplace, as would be sinking 40-foot putts. Ah,
Dad, it would be something else if there were golf
courses in heaven, and again, I'm not going to tell you
with certainty whether there are or aren't.

But you know, Dad, as I reflect on it, I doubt that you'd even choose to play golf here. You'd want to spend your time doing what the rest of us do—worshiping and serving our Lord. What a glorious place this is, and Dad, I know you'll know how to take this, but as much as I love you and the rest of the family, I must confess that I haven't really missed you. I am having a wonderful time here! My exhilaration is so great when I realize that in the twinkling of an eye, you and Mom will be with me, as well as the rest of the family. And, oh, boy, what a magnificent time we will all have then! I can tell you with great authority that if you think the Ziglar family reunions have been exciting and delightful, you don't have a clue as to what a real family reunion is all about!

Until you get here, Dad, I just want to sign off by encouraging you to keep doing the things you do so well and that you love to do so much. Keep on loving Mom as you do, and keep on telling people about Jesus. Then, Dad, when you get to heaven, if the Lord decides to let you make a speech, I can assure you that the acoustics will be perfect, the audience will be wildly enthusiastic, and it will be by far the biggest event you've ever addressed. That's exciting, Dad!

Sure do love you,
Suzan

Even though I wrote this letter to myself, in many ways it truly was a letter from Suzan. It expressed her personality, her ideas, her concern, her enthusiasm. It blessed me to recall Suzan's personality, her love, and her insights. It truly influenced my grief that day—turning it from sadness to joy, from sorrow to delight.

My relationship with my daughter is ongoing, and it will ever be so. She not only lives in heaven, she lives in my heart.

I encourage you to keep your relationship with your loved one renewed and fresh. After all, you both are alive in Christ, and you continue to have Him and so much "history" as well as "future" in common!

15

GOD'S STRENGTH AND
GRACE TO CONTINUE
WITH LIFE AND WORK

As Suzan lay dying in the hospital, I faced the fact that speaking engagements remained on my schedule. They seemed to have been divinely coordinated to a remarkable degree. Even so, there were two engagements that I felt strongly I needed to fulfill. Each involved my going out of town one day and returning the next.

In the case of the first seminar, several thousand people were expected, and I felt Suzan would want me to honor the commitment I had made. The second engagement was not as large, but I felt compelled to fulfill it.

After I finished the second engagement, the phone call came that Suzan had taken a turn for the worse, and I immediately rushed back to Dallas. Bob Alexander, my associate, took my place at the third engagement and did a marvelous job. The following summer, that same organization met in Dallas and I was able to fulfill my commitment to speak to them a year late.

I schedule speaking engagements up to three years in

advance, so I had a strong feeling as I went to the events that were scheduled immediately after Suzan's death that the Lord had arranged these events in His timing. Certainly the Lord who knows all things knew precisely what the situation would be at the time I spoke to the groups.

This knowledge did not make my heart any lighter, and yet I felt God's presence with me in a way that was as real as I have ever felt. In a question-and-answer session at the first event after Suzan's death, I shared with those present the loss of my daughter, my feelings, and my faith. I believe my sharing had a significant impact on many members of that organization, as evidenced by the phone calls and letters I received later. I had a profound understanding as I spoke that God is good, particularly in our most difficult times. Even though I found it extraordinarily difficult to speak with the loss of Suzan so fresh on my mind, I knew the grace of God in a depth that I had never experienced before.

I also came to the realization that the end of one person's ministry on this earth does not, and should not, signal the end of another person's ministry and witness for Christ. It should enhance the ministry and work of others.

The fact that I can continue to live and work, and even continue to live as a more complete person and to do better work, is a testament to Suzan's influence and witness for Christ. It is a tribute to her.

NO GUILT IN CONTINUING TO DO GOD'S BIDDING

About two months after Suzan died, I called Dr. Paige Patterson—not out of distress or anxiety, but out of curiosity.

I was finding that as I went about my daily life, I was thinking about Suzan less, and on the occasions when my thoughts did turn to her, I often deliberately shifted my thinking to issues at hand. In retrospect, I believe I was looking for a little reassurance from Dr. Patterson that what I was doing was normal and not a form of denial.

Dr. Patterson said he had both good news and bad news for me. He said, "The good news is yes, this is normal behavior, and you are not in denial. The bad news is that for the rest of your life, from time to time, memories of Suzan will flood back into your mind, and you will weep and feel the loss of your loved one."

Dr. Patterson went on to explain that he believed this was a part of God's providence in the grieving process. As we grow older, thoughts of our lost loved ones are brought back to memory by a loving God as a part of our preparation to enter eternity. Memories of loved ones who have preceded us in death make us even more aware that our homegoing will be a reunion with all whom we have loved so much on this earth.

I also came to the conclusion that God uses this ability and desire to continue in our work to make us stronger in our faith. To continue to do the work that God has put before us to do is a form of spiritual warfare; it is a statement in the spiritual realm that we will not be defeated in our God-given purpose in life despite what the enemy of our souls might have intended as a stumbling stone or brick wall. In the years since Suzan died, I have talked to a number of people whose ministries have become even more effective after the death of a loved one. These people continued their work, and they did so with greater faith and reliance upon God. And God honored and blessed their expression of trust in Him with incredible results.

Ike Reighard, whom I mentioned earlier, was one such person. Ike felt intense grief; in a mirror of my experience, he seemed to feel the greatest intensity between the third and fourth weeks. But Ike also went on to be used in subsequent years to preach God's Word and praise God in spectacular ways.

In the story of King David's life, there is an incident in which he wept, fasted, and prayed over a son who was born critically ill. When word came to him that his son had died, David responded by saying that he accepted that his son could not come back to live with him, but that one day he would go to be with his son. And then David got up and dried his tears. (See 2 Sam. 12:15–23.) I believe the Lord calls each grieving person to do the same.

Tears will be shed in the days, months, years, and perhaps even decades after the death of a loved one, but in each case, the tears are to be shed and then the person is to get up and dry the tears. There is a good and right season for weeping—a season that may come again and again—but there is also a time for weeping to end. God still has a purpose for our lives that must be fulfilled, and we cannot fulfill it unless we reach the point where our tears have been released and we can again function in strength, in courage, and with a concerted focus on the tasks God has put before us.

GREATER EFFECTIVENESS AND PURPOSE IN MY WORK

One day several months after Suzan's death, I entered my executive assistant's office to hear the excited voice of Kathy Losey, one of our capable saleswomen whose life God has truly used in enhancing my spiritual life. She was saying to Laurie over the speaker phone, "I don't know what's happening to Zig. He's always been great, but it seems that the things he's doing now are better than anything he's ever done." Laurie responded by noting that others in the company had been saying the same thing.

I interrupted at this point, calling Kathy by name. She said, "Zig, are you there?" I said, "Yes, and I need to ask you a question. I want you to tell me the truth. Did you know I was sitting here as you said all that to Laurie?" She laughed and told me that, of course, she hadn't known.

As Laurie and I continued to talk after Kathy hung up, Laurie asked me if I didn't find it frightening at times to know the role I played in some people's lives. I told her that it wasn't frightening to me because I learned long ago that I have no reason to take credit for anything that had happened to me since my forty-fifth birthday. I reminded Laurie that I knew full well that my life was going nowhere prior to my inviting Christ into my life. Comments such as the ones Kathy made only remind me that it is the Lord in me and through me who is accomplishing His purposes. I am grateful to be a vessel He can use. Compliments such as the ones Kathy gives are ones I quickly choose to turn into praises to God.

In reflecting upon what Kathy, Laurie, and others were saying, I recognized that I, too, could see ways in which God was making me more effective in my work.

It is true. I *have* felt God's presence, power, and love in an ever-increasing way. The response when I speak, the letters I receive after I speak, and the comments made by those who attend my seminars all indicate that God has His hand on me and that He is using me in new ways.

Part of what has made me more effective, I believe, is

my awareness that Suzan would want me to do the things I must do.

Knowing that Suzan is with the Lord and is in a far better place than she ever experienced on this earth has done a great deal to energize my efforts to share my faith with more people. How I long for every person to have that assurance about the loved ones who precede him in death! How I long for that truth to apply to every person who dies!

If we have a clear vision of heaven and of God's grace and love that enable eternal life to be possible in the future as well as a present reality, we will want every person we encounter to accept Jesus as Savior.

TODAY IS THE FOUNDATION
FOR TOMORROW

All that has happened in the past is a foundation for today. In my life, my past grieving is part of my current foundation. What I do with today, including the way I choose to grieve, becomes the foundation on which I will stand tomorrow.

We hold quarterly People Builders meetings at Zig Training Systems to recognize the outstanding accomplishments of our people. We always have a testimonial from one of our clients at these events so that our entire staff can be reminded that we are meeting needs of people across the nation. Our guest at one of these meetings was Mark Warren. He shared with the group how at age thirty, he had achieved financial success. He was a millionaire, owned beautiful homes and luxury automobiles, and maintained a lifestyle that would have been envied by many. At the same time, he was aware that he had little interest in people. His heart was hard and his relationships were empty.

On a trip to the Los Angeles area, Mark's clients invited him to accompany them to one of my seminars. He went, expecting to hear the typical hype and New Age promises that he had often heard at motivational seminars. He was stunned to hear me speak of my faith and even use some Bible verses. He was further amazed when I spoke of my love for my wife and the relationship I had with each of my children. He was impressed by the fact that I recognized and acknowledged the importance of the support I received from our staff in putting together seminars and in helping me.

Mark said he felt strangely moved to explore further what I had that he didn't have. That evening he picked up a Gideon Bible in his hotel room and started reading it. He turned to the book of Proverbs and read some of Solomon's wisdom. The next morning, he rose early and drove to the airport, only to be told that the airport was fogged in and no flights would be leaving for several hours. He drove to another airport in the greater Los Angeles area, and when he finally was seated comfortably in his airplane seat, he said that he was just about ready to launch into what would have been his first-ever experience with prayer when he looked up into the face of "the most beautiful person he had ever seen." This woman was one of the flight attendants. She was not just pretty; her eyes were flashingly alive, and her countenance reflected joy, peace, and excitement. He got up, followed her to the back of the plane, and asked her to go out to lunch with him. She responded that she never dated pilots or passengers. Somewhat subdued, he returned to his seat, but he couldn't get her out of his mind.

As he was leaving the plane, he handed her his business card. He confessed to us that his hand was shaking when he handed the card to her, and he told her that he really would like to take her to lunch and he hoped she would give him a call. She did call and explained to him that she did only because his hand was shaking, so he seemed sincere! Later she took him to church with her, and she was the instrument God used to lead him to Christ. Today Margie is his wife and the mother of their two beautiful children.

Margie's second pregnancy, however, was not an easy one. She developed serious medical problems, and the physicians predicted that their baby would be seriously disabled as a result. Abortion was recommended to them, but because of their faith in Christ, that was not an option to them. Their little boy was born in perfect health and has an unusually keen mind as well.

Mark shared this story with us, especially with me, I believe, because he wanted us to know that if it had not been for the message of faith and family love that we presented in the seminar, he would never have married this woman or had the two beautiful children they now have.

All that we do in our faith and from the foundation of our faith eventually bears consequences that are the miracles of God!

In many ways, Suzan's faith-filled life is one more vital stone in the foundation of my faith. And out of the expression of my faith, God can and does work His miracles.

Choose to draw upon the strength of others. Choose to see the strength in the one you love who has died. Choose to move forward on the foundation of strength your loved one has contributed to your life.

MORE COMPLETE AS A HUMAN BEING

Not only has my work been impacted since the death of Suzan, but also my life as a man, a husband, and a father.

Our shared grief has made us more complete and strong as a family.

The Redhead and I have always had a great marriage, and it is even greater today than before Suzan went home to be with the Lord. For that, I am truly thankful.

Statistical reports state that the death of a child often leads parents to divorce courts. The exact opposite has been true for the Redhead and me. I cannot fathom that anybody could have replaced either of us when it came to the help we have given each other in the grieving process. Who but the Redhead knew Suzan from even before her birth, watched every facet of her life, rejoiced in her joy, or worked with her in times of tears and sorrow? Who else could understand the joy we had at proudly showing her off to others?

Recognize as you grieve that your grief will affect all your relationships, especially your marriage relationship. If faith and love are strong in your relationship, grief can make your relationship stronger. If faith and love are weak, your relationship may well be weakened. The kind of relationship you have with another person seems to be *intensified* by grief. I am grateful that our marriage was a strong one and thus is now stronger.

Both my wife and I have a deeper love for our Lord than we had prior to Suzan's death. We have a deeper commitment to serving the Lord in an ever-increasing way. We have a greater appreciation for the beautiful aspects of life and a greater longing for heaven. We have an even greater thankfulness for the wonderful years we had with Suzan and a greater anticipation for the eternity our family will spend together.

In the aftermath of Suzan's homegoing I made a decision about time. I began to reflect upon the many business trips I had been taking, often leaving my family on Sunday afternoons. I thought of all of the times I was telling the Redhead good-bye. And I made the decision that effective immediately, I was going to cut down on my speaking engagements and spend more time at home writing books and articles. I felt that was physically necessary, and the time had come for me to spend more time with my family. I also decided to indulge myself in the luxury of waking up in my own bed, eating at my own table, and doing things that "normal" people do. I included a little more golf in my plans.

My decision regarding time is one that I believe many people make as part of the grieving process. Every moment of every day takes on a little different perspective after the loss of a loved one, and priorities are readjusted.

I have always loved my family, and they have always been a top priority for me. My decision was not only to love my family more—but to *show my love to my family more* by spending more time with them.

How we choose to show our love is just as important, I believe, as the fact that we love.

How we choose to respond, *how* we choose to move forward in our lives, *how* we choose to develop and grow spiritually, and *how* we choose to turn to God in our trust and faith will determine the future effectiveness of our lives and become the final testimony to the influence of the departed loved one on our lives.

God will impart to each of us His strength and grace to do what He has called us to do. It is up to us to choose to continue to walk with boldness and faith the path He unfolds before us.

16

THE LOSS
AND
THE LOVE

YEARS AGO, when I heard of a mother losing a member of her large family, I thought, *Well, at least she still has seven other children.* I realize now what an insensitive and inaccurate thought that was.

There is no doubt that the mother was aware of and grateful for the fact that she had seven living children. However, in no way did the presence of her other children lessen the loss of the one who had died. My wife and I have four children—one in heaven and three on earth. As much as we love and cherish the three children who remain with us on this earth, their presence does not diminish one iota the grief we have felt over the loss of our Suzan. We are truly grateful that we have three children alive on this earth and we love them dearly, but we continue to love Suzan and long for her presence.

On occasion I have thought, as I feel certain many parents have thought, *Which of my children would I rescue if they all were endangered and I could save only one?* I reflected about this one day while I was walking with my daughter Cindy. I told her I knew exactly which child I would save. She looked at me with a puzzled half smile and asked, "Who?"

I responded, "The one I was closest to in the midst of the crisis."

I can't imagine how it would feel to pass over one child to rescue another, especially if all the children were eventually rescued. How would the other children feel in the aftermath of a situation in which I had chosen one over the others? The thought is unthinkable. I am so grateful that not one of my children—or as far as I know, one of my grandchildren—has ever doubted that the love from me or from the Redhead has been anything other than rock-solid secure and wholehearted. We have had no favorites. We love each child differently, but we love each one equally.

This book is about the death of Suzan and the grief we felt after her homegoing. But in no way should any person conclude that our love for Suzan has been magnified by her death to the point that it overshadows our love for our living children. My wife and I love each of our children beyond what words can convey. In no way do we love Suzan more because she has died, and certainly not more in the sense of comparing our love for her to our love for her siblings.

As important as it has been for me to keep my relationship with Suzan alive in my mind and heart, it has also been very important for me to renew other family relationships and to cause them to grow.

One day I phoned the Redhead from the airport right after I had landed to tell her I was on the ground and would be home shortly. She told me that Cindy had been thrown from a horse and had a crushed vertebra. She assured me that her condition was not serious, but that she would be incapacitated to a large degree for a couple of weeks. She experienced no danger of paralysis. Nevertheless, I was deeply concerned and somewhat shaken.

After losing Suzan, it seems that every person I love has become even more dear to me. Although I don't believe that I actually love them more than I did before, I am more aware of my love for them and the place they occupy in my heart.

The thought quickly came, as you might suspect, *Cindy could have been left paralyzed or killed.* I praised God that He had not permitted either outcome to happen.

Almost immediately, we all adjusted to the fact that Cindy needed our care. Her husband's responsibilities at work were relegated only to the "gotta do it now" category. If Cindy's condition had been worse, there wouldn't have been *any* gotta-do-it-nows. All of our priorities were placed on what we could do to help Cindy.

No, our love for Cindy was not greater during that time, but her need for us was greater, and we were even more mindful of our need for her and our love for her—and how life and health hang by a thin thread.

This is the way it is, I believe, when we lose someone to death. We become immediately aware of how much we loved that person, and we are also more aware of the many ways in which he needed us and we needed him—in other words, of the bonds of the relationship we enjoyed.

I have heard of instances, however, in which a "lost child" has been elevated to near sainthood in the minds and hearts of those left behind, sometimes to the neglect and to the diminishment of the value of the children and loved ones who remain alive. The very thought breaks my heart.

Every child is unique and irreplaceable, and deserves to

be loved unconditionally with all of a parent's heart. That love does not end in death, but neither should love for the "lost child" be expressed to the point of neglecting to express and show love for the remaining children.

THE RELATIONSHIP BETWEEN
LOSS AND LOVE

How does the love that a parent has for a child impact the grief that is felt over the loss of that child? I'm certain that all parents who have suffered the loss of a child agree that the deeper the love for the child, the deeper the grief.

When I think about the love we all have and had for Suzan, I am reminded of several instances in which men and women have said to me that never again would they give themselves completely to a love because they had loved and lost and found they didn't handle the loss well. They were sincere in what they were saying. There is a vast difference, however, between the love a parent feels for a child lost in death and the love a man and a woman might feel for each other in a romantic relationship. In the loss of a child to death, there is no way in which a truly loving parent can turn off that love or say, "I wish I had never loved." Rather, the grieving parent is wise to rejoice in the fact that he has loved, that he does love, and that he will continue to love. Love does not die with death.

My heart goes out to people who have never loved so deeply that they feel the loss of another person in every fiber of their bodies. That is an indication to me that their relationships have not been marked by deep love, and oh, how much they have missed by not experiencing deep love! Should we love any less because the depth of love is inevitably linked to the depth of pain and grief we might feel at the loss of a child? Certainly not!

No parent begrudges the fact that he loved his children to the utmost of his capacity to love. The same should be true for the love between spouses and other family members. Love is a vital ingredient of life.

I vividly recall when our second daughter, Cindy, was born. I could not imagine prior to her birth that I could possibly love another child in our family as much as I loved our firstborn. The matter was of considerable concern to me when I realized that a second child was on the way. I confess that I carried the concern about my capacity to love a second child equally right up until the instant I saw our beautiful Cindy and held her in my arms. My love for her was immediate and complete and without measure. When Julie and Tom came along, those thoughts about my capacity to love never entered my mind because I knew that I not only could, but *would,* love them just as much as I loved Suzan and Cindy.

On the other side of grief is the joy that the Redhead and I experienced at Suzan's birth. We knew full well that Suzan was a gift from God. The joy we felt at her appearance was and is unspeakable; our gratitude to God is overwhelming. Because we understand that Suzan was a gift from God, we can more readily understand and accept the fact that she was on loan to us. We were to love and cherish her, and to provide and care for her, which we did throughout her life. Now her heavenly Father has called her home where He will provide love and care for her in an infinitely better way than we ever dreamed possible. We did the best we could, but God is God and can do so much more.

If someone were to ask me whether we still would have

wanted Suzan to be born, knowing prior to her birth that she would go home to heaven at age forty-six, my answer would be, "Yes, of course! A thousand times yes!"

The joy and happiness Suzan brought into our lives are immeasurable. The memories she left behind are valuable beyond calculation. The two precious children and the wonderful husband she brought into our family are dearly loved and appreciated. The contributions Suzan made while she was with us are numberless.

My life and the lives of all those who knew Suzan were enriched by her presence among us. We will be eternally grateful that we were privileged to know her and love her for forty-six years.

THE AMAZING THING ABOUT LOVE

We cannot fully comprehend two amazing facts about love. First, love is intended to be given. It cannot be stored up. If you truly want to have a lot of love, you must continually give a lot of love. And second, as Paul wrote in his first letter to the Corinthians, "love never fails" (1 Cor. 13:8 NKJV). Nothing satisfies the human heart as much as love does.

When we pour love into our children, we do not expect to withdraw this love from them. We love them because they are ours, and we cannot help loving them! The Redhead and I poured our love into Suzan all of her life, and we are so grateful that we did.

Our grief has been directly linked to the fact that we have loved Suzan through the years with a generosity of heart and a depth of love I cannot convey in words. Does that mean that I wish we had loved her less so that the grief I have felt would be less? Certainly not!

The truth is, if we do not express deep love for a person, we are likely to experience substantial guilt at his passing. We will have our minds and hearts filled with "if only," "what if," and "I wish I had" conjectures. Guilt also creates grief. Of the two I would much rather have loved deeply and lost the one I loved than to have loved less, lost the one I loved through death, and then have felt the pangs of guilt.

I once read this quote from an anonymous source: "What a man does for himself, he takes with him; what he does for others, he leaves behind." How true.

Cindy described Suzan as the most unselfish person she had ever known. As people from across our nation have shared their favorite Suzan memories through letters, calls, and statements to us, I have been amazed at the legacy of love and caring she left. Another quote comes to mind: "The tragedy of life is not that love ends so soon, but that we wait so long to begin to love." I am grateful that Suzan didn't wait in expressing her love. And that we didn't wait or withhold our love either. I encourage you not to wait or withhold your love.

17

WHY WE FEEL
NO REGRET AND
NO GUILT

JUST BEFORE CHRISTMAS in 1995, I was listening one afternoon to one of John Maxwell's "Injoy Life" tapes as I baby-sat our newest granddaughter, Alexandra. John was talking about people who had failed in life, and then he quoted Mother Teresa, who said, "Failure is the kiss of Jesus." Someone asked her what she meant, and she replied, "When we ourselves fail, then we turn to Jesus." It was a poignant thought that caused me to reflect on some of the failing moments I had experienced or witnessed in my life.

As my thoughts turned to Suzan's homegoing, I came to the conclusion that in no way did I believe the doctors, nurses, or medical community had failed Suzan. Their professionalism, medical expertise, and loving, caring approach combined to produce the best care available. We believe they did everything they could do, and their sense of loss was great also. The attending physician had tears in his eyes at Suzan's death.

Neither do I believe that our Christian brothers and sisters failed in their prayers or that we failed in our prayers as a family.

The need for prayer was sent out over several Internet organizations, which reach more than a million people. Prayer services were held for Suzan in India, Jerusalem, many cities of Canada, and cities and towns across the United States. Prayer circles, Sunday school classes, churches, customers, friends—people from literally every walk of life—prayed fervently for Suzan. All asked for a miracle from God, but those who truly know Jesus Christ as Savior were also praying for God's will. In my case and in the case of my family, we were praying that God's will would be a miracle. We felt that Suzan still had so much to give and to do. We could see so many who needed her influence, her joy, and her unselfish giving. My prayers were that God might let her live so that she could make an even greater contribution to the world. I prayed that the Lord would allow her to serve Him for many more years.

For those who do not understand anything about God and the Christian walk, I can imagine that their first response would be to scoff and say, "God doesn't really hear prayers. And if He hears them, He doesn't answer."

That thought never crossed my mind as I prayed, and as far as I know, it never entered the minds of any members of our family. In some ways, Suzan was more mature in her Christian walk than we were in that she trusted God fully both to hear prayer and to answer it *in His way and in His timing.*

As much as our society as a whole may seem to deny or ignore God, I believe strongly that every time a person finds himself in a desperate, life-threatening, or so-called hopeless situation, that person will instinctively and invariably turn to God. Although the media may not reflect this pervasive underlying faith, statistical studies have shown that 96 percent of all Americans believe God exists, 91 percent pray each week, and the "nonbelievers" indicate that they call on God in life-threatening situations, just in case He exists!

We called upon God repeatedly during Suzan's illness.

What should our response be when we pray and God doesn't give us the answer we want? Is there still something miraculous for us to see? The answer is yes!

God has several options when it comes to answering our prayers. He can say yes, no, not now, or perhaps. It is no less an answer to prayer when God says no. However, when God answers our prayers in a way that is different from what we had hoped, we can trust that God knows a better way and He has chosen to initiate a better plan. In Suzan's death, we saw God saying to us, "Suzan is better off with Me. I love her so much that I have chosen to do what is best for her."

Both medically and spiritually, we did all that we could and all that God had asked us to do. There was no failure.

The reality was, as the psalmist once wrote, that God had numbered Suzan's days and when her purpose on this earth was fulfilled, God took her home to be with Him.

WILLING TO ACCEPT GOD'S BEST PLAN

On several occasions Suzan said that she knew my inherent optimism and faith would lead me to assure her daughter Katherine that God was going to heal Suzan and restore her to good health. Suzan quietly, lovingly, but also very firmly said to me, "Dad, we just don't know that. We do know that God is sovereign and that our purpose in life is to praise and worship Him. If God chooses to heal me and let me stay with my family to raise my girls, I will rejoice. If He chooses to *really* heal me and call me home, I will rejoice at that. But, Dad, we just don't know God's will in this, and I don't want my fifteen-year-old daughter mad at God because He took her mother home."

How right she was! In her sixteen-year walk with Christ, Suzan had pursued God's Word and had sought His will in every phase of her life. She truly was the "happy Christian" I had written about in the book that God used to claim her for His kingdom. Her advice to me was obviously on target. God did choose to call Suzan home. And I am grateful that Suzan cautioned me in the way she did.

As we look back over the last months and weeks of Suzan's life, most of us in the family have recognized that Suzan knew she would soon be at home with the Lord. She communicated this to us in many ways. The last Christmas she was with us, she gave each family member gifts that were more beautiful and more meaningful than ever. At the time, I wondered if she had made the wisest use of her and her family's resources in her gift giving that Christmas. Now, of course, I see clearly that she knew what she was doing all along.

When Suzan showed improvement after being admitted to Plano Hospital and put on oxygen, those who casually observed her might have thought that she was in denial about her condition. She was doing her utmost to lift us up, encourage us, and we spent hours talking with her and laughing with her. When the decision was made to move her to St. Paul's Medical Center because of its excellent lung transplant team, Suzan laughed and said that if they took her by ambulance, she wanted all the sirens blasting so that everybody would know she was coming. As it turned out, her condition was far more serious than we had realized, and she was transported by CareFlight helicopter.

IGNORANCE *IS* GOOD AT TIMES

Less than a month after Suzan's death, my wife and I were enjoying a quiet, leisurely breakfast at the beautiful Madison Hotel in Washington, D.C., when I commented on the beautiful earrings she was wearing. She smiled and reminded me that I had given them to her the previous Christmas! The memory brought tears to my eyes when I suddenly recalled that I had bought those earrings on the last Christmas shopping spree I was to have with Suzan.

Every year just a few days before Christmas, Suzan and I went shopping for the Redhead. It seemed that Suzan had a talent for finding a few items that she knew her mother would enjoy, and she was always correct.

The last Christmas Suzan was with us, her health was deteriorating, although none of us knew just how much. She was coughing quite a bit, and her energy level was low. Because she didn't seem to feel well, I debated asking her to go with me. I will be eternally grateful that I did call and ask her if she felt like going on our annual shopping spree. Without a moment's hesitation, she said, "Absolutely!"

We went to the shopping center where Suzan loved to shop, and as always, we hit the jackpot. She found some things that her mother really loved and still cherishes. And we enjoyed our time together. We had a long, quiet lunch, and to be candid, I can't recall a single thing we discussed. The lunch was truly one of those pleasant, meaningful experiences that become an integral part of the ongoing relationship enjoyed by a father and a daughter who love each other.

The question has arisen, "Would we have liked to have known sooner that we had such a short time remaining with Suzan?" For me, the answer is, "No, definitely not."

The last few months we had with Suzan included some of the happiest times we shared. Had we known of her impending death, every family get-together would have been clouded by that fact. We probably would have been extra careful not to talk about her coming death. We likely would have tried too hard to have a good time and to do a host of other "unnatural" things, solely because we knew she was ill and we were concerned about her survival. At the time Suzan's illness was first diagnosed, the physicians predicted that she would have four or five years of health before a transplant would be necessary. That was the knowledge in which we were living during her last few months, and overall, we were a concerned but relaxed and happy family. Suzan was as happy as I had ever seen her.

God does have a plan, and it is infinitely better than any plan we could create. I praise God that He is in control because His ways are higher than our ways. (See Isa. 55:9.)

DEALING WITH GUILT

Although the Redhead and I truly feel no regret and no guilt related to Suzan, I know there are parents who bear tremendous guilt in the aftermath of a child's death. For whatever reason, they might never have developed a close relationship with their children. Perhaps they neglected to spend time with them, or perhaps because of circumstances largely beyond their control, they were unable to spend much time with them. Or they might have said or done things they wish they hadn't said or done. They blame themselves and even feel they might have contributed to the child's death in some way. Still others might never have taken the opportunity to express the depth of the love they had for the child. Under those circumstances, the death of a child brings feelings of keen guilt and grief that penetrate the very soul.

If you happen to fit into any of these categories, let me comfort you as best I can with three thoughts.

First, most of us as parents do the best we can with what we know at the time certain situations arise. Remind yourself that you have done the best you knew to do at the time you were raising your child.

Second, none of us can do anything to change anything that has happened in the past. Fortunately, you can choose to let the past teach you. Hanging on to guilt does nothing to benefit the lost loved one and will negatively impact your future and possibly damage your relationship with the remaining family. Rather than nurse guilt, you are wise to recognize and learn from the lesson in the past and to make a renewed commitment to expressing love and showing attention and affection to the children and other loved ones who remain alive.

Third, keep in mind that you were not the sole influence on your child's life. One day after the Redhead and I had been to Suzan's grave, I reflected with my wife that I believed the first years and the last years of Suzan's life were her happiest. She had some difficulties in between, but our joy comes in knowing that Suzan had wonderful growing-up years and in that, we did our work as parents well. We also have abundant joy in knowing that Suzan finished her life well, with courage, faith, dignity, and the blessed assurance that all was well with her soul. That, we know, was the work of the Lord in her life, and it was the result of her faith in and commitment to Jesus Christ.

When you are contemplating the death of someone you dearly love, keep in mind that you have had *your part* in that loved one's life, and the Lord has had His part. You cannot and could not do the Lord's part. The Lord would not do your part.

GUILT RELATED TO UNFORGIVENESS

Suzan had a close friend whom she loved and trusted. Suzan was her confidante, and she supported and helped this friend in many ways. Then suddenly this friend turned on Suzan and said some hurtful things to her. The turn of events baffled Suzan, but she only allowed it to affect her temporarily. She knew that she personally had done nothing to damage the relationship.

The day after Suzan's death, my wife and one of our daughters ran into this particular person who approached them with tears and said, "Oh, I am so glad to see you! I wanted so many times to go to Suzan and ask her to forgive me for what I had done and said to her. Now it's too late, and I regret so much that I didn't go to her."

The woman was heartbroken. The Redhead assured her that long ago Suzan had completely forgiven her. Knowing that might have given her some relief, but she would have felt far less guilt had she gone to Suzan and asked for forgiveness to mend the relationship. It seems there were circumstances in the woman's personal life that caused her to treat Suzan as she had. She said Suzan had done nothing to injure the friendship.

My message to you is simple: do everything in your power to build and maintain good relationships with those whose paths you cross. If a relationship is broken, particularly if you have had a part in the breaking of it, go to the person and ask for forgiveness. Seek to mend the relationship, and *do it now.* A major burden will lift from your heart, and you will avoid an even greater buildup of guilt or bitterness. If someone has wronged you, forgive that person and if humanly possible tell him you have forgiven him. Resentment toward another person becomes acid in the human soul and takes a toll on your life. There is no substitute for knowing that you have done the right thing by other people.

If you need to forgive someone, do it today. If you need to ask for someone's forgiveness, don't delay. Guilt is a by-product of unforgiveness.

CHOOSE TO EXPRESS
YOUR LOVE OPENLY

As I talked to Suzan and read the Bible to her at her bedside, I found myself saying what I had told her hundreds, even thousands of times before: "Suzan, I love you." I badly wanted to tell her one more time of my love and my devotion to her. I wanted those to be the last words she heard from me. I am grateful that she was completely lucid for much of this communication and that I knew with certainty that she was able to comprehend all I said to her.

Spend time with those you love; that is an unspoken way of saying, "I love you." Your presence is a gift of love to a person who loves you in return.

One small but interesting comment that my daughter Julie made to me after Suzan's death was this: "You know, Dad, one of the things I'm most grateful for is that I quit smoking six months before Suzan's hospitalization. Not once did I have to leave my sister's side to smoke a cigarette. Not once did I have to excuse myself from any family discussion to go outside and smoke. Since all of those times were so precious, it means everything to me to have been there for every moment of the experience we went through as a family."

Julie went on to say, "On the Friday night when the doctor first told us that Suzan had only a matter of hours to live, I put my left hand under Suzan's hand and my right hand on top of hers, and I sat there by her bed for three hours, just holding her hand, loving her, talking to her, and thinking about her. That was such a precious time, and I'm so grateful I spent it with my sister." Julie has no "what ifs," no "if onlys," no regrets.

If you can't see your loved ones often, call or write them frequently.

Above all, tell those you love that you love them! I do not recall concluding any phone conversation or visit with Suzan in which I did not tell her that I loved her, and she, in turn, told me that she loved me. Even if we had been apart for only a few hours, I always gave her a hug when I came back into her presence, and she reciprocated enthusiastically. Most of the time I also kissed her as a part of my greeting.

It is impossible for me to tell you how much that means to me now that Suzan is gone. I am grateful for the openly loving and affectionate relationship we had as father and daughter.

Only a few seconds are needed to tell someone, "I love you." But spoken from a sincere heart, these words can mean so much. My heart tells me a person can never hear that message too often.

CHOOSE TO DO MORE
OF THE RIGHT THINGS

While I do not have regrets about my relationship with Suzan, there are some things that I would do more of if I could relive our time together.

I would call her on the phone more often and talk with her at greater length. I would hug and kiss her more every time I was in her presence. I would tell her more frequently of the depth of my love for her. I would ask for and listen more intently to some of her insights. And most of all I would make it a point to spend more time with her.

I also wish that I had taken more close-up photographs of Suzan and close-up shots of her with the members of her precious family. It never occurred to us through the years that of the hundreds of photographs we have of our family members, very few of them are close-ups that show facial features clearly. I encourage you to take such photos of every person you love and then to write the date on the back of each photo.

Please understand that, with the exception of taking close-up photographs, I did all of these things that I've cited while Suzan was alive. In retrospect, however, I wish I had done more of the right things. I see so many people who still have their sons, daughters, parents, brothers, sisters, and friends—people whom they deeply and dearly love— but they do not choose to spend time with their loved ones, talk freely to them of their love, or express their love openly with hugs and kisses. Virtually every person who has lost a loved one to death wishes he had another chance to do *more* of the right things with the lost one. It is painful to the grieving person to see others ignore their loved ones or treat them in unloving ways.

I'd hazard a guess that if you could go back and relive time spent with a departed loved one, you would never forget a birthday, anniversary, Valentine's Day, Christmas, or other important family holiday. I'll bet you would make it a point to make more phone calls and surprise visits. I once dropped in on Suzan for a surprise visit two days in a row.

The delight in her eyes was special to me, but it was also sad in a way since the expression of joy in her eyes told me that I was not talking enough with her or spending enough time with her. Later, Chad made it a point to tell me that those two days were among the best days of her life. I wish I had made more such visits.

Let me encourage you, as a parent, husband, wife, brother, or sister, to go down your list of precious family members and dear friends and ask yourself, When did I last talk with this person? When did I last spend time with him? When did I last encourage this one I love? When did I last tell this person, "I love you"? Life is uncertain, and we don't know when we might lose a child, parent, sibling, or friend who is important to us. Seize the moment. Take the time. Make the effort. And do it now!

During the last few months of Suzan's life, she worked with me closely on the newspaper column. I talked with her or saw her almost daily. After she was gone, one of my other daughters told me that Suzan had commented before she went into the hospital—and before any of us realized fully just how seriously ill she was—that I had called and talked with her *every day for the last ten days* she worked with me. My daughter said that there were sheer delight and joy in Suzan's voice as she shared that bit of information with her sister.

That comment from Suzan, relayed by another of my daughters, made me feel good. At the same time, it made me wish that I had made more calls. I would like to have called her every day for the last ten years of her life!

Now I am not whipping myself for failure in this area. The fact is that I spent a considerable amount of time with Suzan. I'm saying that a two-minute phone call, a five-minute stopover and a note in the mail are such simple things to do, and they are things every person *can* do more frequently.

One of my delights now as I look back over my life and Suzan's life is that I do not have a need to say, "If only I had." I'm certainly not claiming to be a perfect father, but I do believe that all of my children and grandchildren have known from birth that I love them very much. I have done my best to express my love in ways they could experience it and know it with certainty. My wishes are not for things that I did *not* do; rather, my wishes are that I might have done more of the things I did. Suzan's loss has been so great to me in part because I enjoyed so much being with her. I only wish I could have been with her *more.*

No person need have either regret or guilt in the aftermath of a loved one's death. The choices we make now will influence how we feel should we lose a loved one.

18

ONGOING
AFTERSHOCKS
OF GRIEF

MORE THAN THREE years have passed since Suzan died, and grief still shows up at the most unexpected times. A little girl at play might remind me of Suzan's childhood. A beautiful hymn in church, particularly one that calls the name of Jesus, still brings tears—sometimes a flood of them—because it reminds me that she is with Him and my love for her and my grieving for her are freshened.

For me, grief seems to come in waves. It has been more intense at times, less intense at others. For the Redhead, who considered Suzan her closest friend as well as her eldest daughter, the sense of grief has been more constant and abiding.

SOME MOMENTS
MIGHT BE ANTICIPATED

One of my most difficult days of grief came about a month after Suzan died. The Redhead, Cindy, Julie, and I went to the cemetery to visit Suzan's grave, and when I saw the bare ground under which her body lies—no grass yet growing on it—the stark reality of her recent death hit me all over again. In retrospect, that was a moment of recurring grief that I might have anticipated.

Also as might have been expected, December 19, 1995, was a very difficult day for me. December 19 was the date each year that Suzan and I went shopping for her mother's Christmas gifts. It was a highlight of the year for me. We always had a marvelous time looking, laughing, shopping, talking—it was one of those father-daughter things we both enjoyed immensely. We typically ended up at the Galleria Shopping Mall, and after doing our shopping, we went to the Westin Hotel's dining facility that opens onto the mall portion of the Galleria overlooking the ice-skating rink. There we had a pleasant, leisurely lunch and reminisced about our shopping and other moments in the past year. Suzan was an avid listener, an insightful thinker, and an interesting conversationalist.

On that date in 1995, just about seven months after Suzan died, my daughters Cindy and Julie went with me. Their mother had already told them some of the things she wanted for Christmas, and we were able to get them as well as a few other items I wanted her to have. I felt fine as we shopped, but then as we sat down for lunch and I asked the blessing, I was so overcome with how much I loved Jesus, and how much I loved Suzan who was now with Jesus, that I couldn't hold back the tears. My heart was broken anew. The three of us reflected about Suzan's life in heaven, but lunch was a bittersweet time for us.

Some of the other I-should-have-seen-that-coming moments of deep grief have been these:

- The first Christmas Sunday after Suzan died, and especially so as the beautiful hymns of faith were sung. It seems anytime a song is sung about the Lord, my grief is triggered in a fresh way. I automatically and instinctively realize that my Suzan is forever with Him, and while I glory in that fact, I also ache for the void left in my life.

- Father's Day. Father's Day has always been a special holiday in our family. The first Father's Day after Suzan died, however, was excruciatingly painful for me. All of the songs that were sung in church that day reminded me of Suzan. The one thing that kept the day from being an entirely sad one was the powerful and inspiring sermon that Associate Pastor Neal Jeffrey preached from Psalm 63:1, a verse he paraphrased to say, "God, You are my everything— You are my all." He emphasized that God is bigger than anything, even death. I had the distinct feeling that his words were aimed specifically at our family. As always when God's Word is preached truthfully with conviction, people walked the aisles to profess their faith in Christ, and as some youngsters came forward that day, particularly one young lad of about thirteen, I found myself rejoicing. I felt comfort in my heart in realizing that another soul was heavenbound.

As much as these might be anticipated moments for grief to appear, there is little that can be done to avert them or to prepare for them. Perhaps the only thing that can be done to prepare for such moments is to have loved ones with you to help bear the burden of sorrow.

UNEXPECTED MOMENTS OF SORROW

There have been other moments of deep grief, however, that I was unable to anticipate.

One was an episode of the television series *Touched by an Angel* in which a fourteen-year-old girl died of cystic fibrosis. Since the girl was an Elvis fan, the angel of death in the program played an Elvis recording of "Precious Lord" as the child died. I found myself with a flood of tears while recalling the exact moment God called Suzan home.

And when I watch a parent pick up a little girl and hug her tightly, I invariably think, *I once picked up Suzan and loved her just as that parent is doing.* I long to be able to hold my little girl again.

There are also times when I seem to have flashbacks of her presence with us, such as on Easter Sunday and at family anniversary and birthday parties. A phrase, a scene, an aroma, a feeling—all have the potential to evoke fresh memories of Suzan, and with the fresh memories grief returns. There is no way to avoid these times unless one hardens one's heart against all feeling, and that would be a miserable way to live and one that I am certain is displeasing to God. I much prefer to remain sensitive, aware, and loving, even if I feel occasional pain.

The good news always is that when these moments of sorrow reappear—expectedly or unexpectedly—the Lord is always present to help me through them.

THE ODD ABSENCE OF GRIEF AT TIMES

The strange nature of grief also has this oddity: there have been moments in which I *expected* to experience grief and strong memories, and yet those moments passed without strong emotion or, in some cases, without remembrance. This happened to me on May 11 the year after Suzan died. I awoke at five o'clock in the morning with Suzan very much on my mind. I was keenly aware that the one-year anniversary of her going home to be with the Lord was approaching on May 13.

Strangely enough, the day before had been Suzan's birthday, and it had not been until the evening of May 10, when a friend of Suzan's called to say she had been thinking about Suzan on her birthday, that I even recalled what the date meant to us. I had been so focused on 9:45 A.M., May 13—the time Suzan died—that I had completely forgotten 2:23 A.M., May 10, the time of her birth. Perhaps that is our nature, to forget the things for which we have been so grateful and to focus our thoughts instead on what we have lost and what has caused us tears and heartache.

As difficult as the first Father's Day was for me after Suzan's death, I couldn't help anticipating that our July Fourth celebration might be equally difficult since it was only the second family holiday get-together without Suzan. The day had a general sadness to it, but it was not nearly as painful as Father's Day had been. We all gathered at Julie's home, and for most of the day, were surrounded by children, grandchildren, in-laws, and close friends. We had a wonderful time talking and playing horseshoes. By day's end, I was thankful to God that we had enjoyed a time marked by laughter, shared tears, and fun.

Yet another occasion that I had thought might be difficult but didn't turn out to be was the celebration of my seventieth birthday, which was followed closely by the celebration of our fiftieth wedding anniversary.

On my birthday, the folks at the company put together a surprise party at a local cafeteria. Laughter and a little speech making from Laurie Magers, my executive assistant, and Bryan Flanagan, one of our outstanding speakers, were part of the event. The family was there, as were virtually all of the employees. We had a delicious meal, a birthday cake, and a short thank-you from me.

Later that afternoon daughters Julie and Cindy came by and prepared my birthday dinner. Once the major part of the work was done, I took a brisk thirty-minute walk with my daughters, and we had a great time talking, laughing, and sharing. The rest of the family joined us for dinner, and there were presents and laughter. For years Suzan had baked her pecan cookies for such occasions. This year, Cindy had found the recipe and baked a big batch of them for me.

As always, Suzan was a part of our conversations, and with a mixture of laughter and tears, we were reminded she is no longer with us for these happy times. We wondered aloud if perhaps she was listening and watching us, and we felt certain that if she was, she was commenting on the fact that Cindy had done well with the pecan cookies but they weren't quite up to her perfection. After stating this, she would have given a hearty laugh.

As family members from all over the Southeast as well as Washington, D.C., and other areas began to gather for our fiftieth wedding anniversary celebration, Suzan was obviously conspicuous by her absence. But it was amazing to me that each time Suzan's name came up, it was generally with a speculation about what Suzan would say or do if she were present.

Two of the conclusions that I have drawn from all of these experiences are these:

1. *Grief emerges at random.* It resurfaces often when one least expects it. There is no predicting the course that grief will take or the moments when it will reappear in one's life.

2. *Grief may subside, but it never fully departs.* From time to time a fleeting thought passes through my mind that I am pretty well over my grief. No sooner does that thought enter my mind, however, than I realize I am just kidding myself. Though the grief has subsided, it has not disappeared entirely. It will always be present to a degree because I will always love Suzan and will always choose to have vivid memories of her.

MEMORIES CANNOT BE SEPARATED FROM FEELINGS

I have come to accept the fact that if I am to retain strong memories of Suzan, which I desire to do, then I am going to have feelings related to the memories. Memories cannot be separated from feelings. And some of the feelings are likely to be a mixture of sadness and pain at the realization that while memories are wonderful, I can no longer make new memories with Suzan.

My sweet memories of Suzan, my love for her, and my delight in having had her as my first baby, then my little girl, later my conversational buddy, ultimately my business associate, and finally my role model–teacher make every second of grieving worth any pain that may come. I have too many fond memories of Suzan to desire that they leave my mind completely. If the price of memories—good, sweet, loving, and vivid—is the price of grief, then I choose to experience grief.

Nevertheless, sometimes strong memories do not automatically evoke grief, and I am grateful for those times. One such time was after I had taken Lisa McInnis-Smith to the airport for her return flight to her native Australia. She and her family have been guests in our home a number of times, and the most recent two-day visit with Lisa had been particularly meaningful. She is completely sold out to serving our Lord, and it's beautiful to listen to her describe the ministry that she and her husband, Colin, share.

As I was returning home from the airport, I was listening to a tape from Focus on the Family—a presentation by Mrs. Patricia Ashley who spoke about marriage and its sanctity as a gift from God. She spoke about love and life, commitment and responsibility, and the joy and beauty that are all aspects of a God-ordained marriage.

In her discussion of life, she referred to abortion as being a heinous crime and a major problem in our society. She encouraged those who had experienced an abortion to seek the forgiveness of God to bring about peace and healing in their lives. She spoke about how Elizabeth's baby leaped with joy in her womb at the sound of Mary's voice and how Elizabeth had exclaimed that Mary was "blessed among women."

Hearing those words, I was reminded with a flood of memories about how incredibly blessed my wife and I felt at the news we were to have a baby. As a young couple, we were thrilled that we were going to be trusted with a baby, and that baby, of course, was Suzan. Frankly I heard very little of what Mrs. Ashley said after that. My thoughts for the remainder of my drive home were filled with memories of Suzan. Those memories were not sad—rather, they were joy-filled memories of her arrival, her babyhood, and her young years growing up.

A ROLLER-COASTER TRUTH
ABOUT GRIEF

We are all familiar with the statement "What goes up must come down." Equally true is the statement "What goes down *can* go up!"

At times, grief seems to have something of a roller-coaster impact on my life. I recall one day about four weeks after Suzan's death. On this particular day, I had played golf, and even played well, which always makes me feel good. When I returned home from the golf course, I found our granddaughters Keeper and Little Lover in the swimming pool. Julie Jackson, Elizabeth's nanny, was nearby, as were Cindy and our friend Lisa Burrus and her two daughters. They all were having a wonderful poolside time. I had a sandwich and soda as I chatted with these guests and played with my granddaughters. We dealt with a few problems related to the adjustments we were all facing as Suzan's parents, sister, mother, and friend. We each had a few sad and reflective thoughts, but overall, it was a happy time.

Later that evening, the Redhead shared an instance that had occurred between Julie and Elizabeth. Elizabeth, as perhaps only a mentally disabled child can say, had noted to Julie, "Mommy's sick. Mommy has gone to heaven." Hearing these words made my heart ache, and I found myself grieving again.

The roller coaster that had been climbing upward all day suddenly came rushing down its track.

223

Just as assuredly, however, the next morning was a new day entirely. The sadness of the evening before had passed.

This up-down-up-again nature of grief seems to be the normal process for most people who have lost loved ones. Rather than see grief as something to be avoided, I choose to concentrate on the fact that the Lord always has a means of comfort and an expression of joy to compensate for each time of sadness or sorrow.

One of the times when I seem to experience grief the most is also the time when God brings me the greatest joy. This generally happens when I am sitting in church, studying my Bible, praying, or preparing my Sunday school lesson. When I am grieving, I instinctively know that it is natural and that grief is working its way, however slowly, through its process. At this time, there are still valleys where the grief seems to hit the hardest on Sundays. But I can face the grief with eternal hope and say, "It's okay"—because it is well with my soul; it's my heart that is hurting.

A number of hymns evoke waves of grief in me. Not only does the music open me up emotionally, but I hear the lyrics of these songs with "new ears" since Suzan has passed away. Music has a special way of tugging at the heart and often brings on tears along with feelings of joy, love, and gratitude.

One such day was Sunday, March 16, 1997, almost two years after Suzan died. That Sunday morning was particularly difficult for me. The Redhead was unable to be with me in church because she was recuperating from foot surgery. My son, Tom, was not there, so I was in church without my family, who mean so much to me. Our choir sang "In the Presence of Jehovah," and the song evoked a flood of images of Suzan, who is truly "in the presence of Jehovah." That evening, as the Redhead and I watched an episode of *Touched*

by an Angel that dealt with the love of family, I was again overcome with a sense of grief and loneliness for Suzan.

Three days later, I found myself reading the eleventh
chapter of John's Gospel. John recorded the words of Jesus:
"I am the resurrection and the life. Those who believe in
me, even though they die like everyone else, will live again"
(John 11:25 NLT). Just as deep as the grief I had felt on
Sunday, in my heart and soul I knew that Suzan believed in
Christ with all her heart. She knew that He is sovereign, that
He is God, and because of this, she now knows that Jesus *is*
"the resurrection and the life." She is not dead, but alive. I
felt a peace of mind and a profound sense of gratitude that
all is well with Suzan.

Toward the end of John 11, Jesus called Lazarus from
the grave and said to others standing nearby, "Unwrap him
and let him loose." Suzan again came to mind, and I realized anew that Suzan has been "unwrapped." She truly is
"loosed" from all pain and is worshiping our Lord with full
freedom of motion and spirit in the Lord's presence. What
a comfort it was to me to again know deep in my spirit that
she is not suffering, but is worshiping, praising, and rejoicing with our Lord. Almost as suddenly as I had felt overcome by grief, my faith, hope, and joy moved upward again.

Yes, the unexpected moments of grief bring sorrow, but
the unexpected moments of comfort and joy from the Lord
overcome the sorrow.

OPPOSITES ARE PART OF OUR HUMAN EXPERIENCE

In *Fiddler on the Roof,* Tevia says on several occasions, "On
the one hand . . . ," only to say almost immediately, "But on

the other hand . . ." Most of us can relate fully to his predicaments. On the one hand, I could have stopped going to church or stopped listening to the great hymns of the church, and I might have shed fewer tears in grief. On the other hand, that would have been the wrong thing to do. My joy would have been limited, and my healing from grief's pain would have been stifled.

In many ways, our Christian experience is a dilemma. On the one hand, I long to be with Christ in heaven and to be with those I love who have gone before me in death. On the other hand, I desire to live as long as possible with those I love on this earth.

Suzan experienced these same feelings in the last days of her life.

About a week before Suzan died, Cindy asked her if she was ready to go to heaven. She nodded her head indicating yes. Then Cindy asked her if she wanted to go, and she shook her head no. Her sister then asked Suzan a third question—whether she wanted to stay and be with us, and again she nodded yes. There is no doubt in my mind that Suzan clearly understood the gravity of her situation. She knew she was at death's door, and while she was prepared to meet Christ, she did not want to leave her family. By the time the last week of her life had passed, however, I feel certain that she was fully ready to be with the Lord.

And isn't that the way we all feel? We long to be with the Lord, but we don't want to leave loved ones. We are eager to reach the destination of life's journey, and yet we are not eager to leave behind those who walk life's road.

My grief has known this same two-sided reality. On the one hand, I have sorrow; on the other, abundant joy.

Merton and Irene Stromman have written in their book

Five Cries of Grief that grief "touches a minor chord that throughout one's life will interpenetrate the jubilant major chords of life, giving greater depth to one's love and appreciation of family and friends." That certainly has been my experience.

I still grieve about Suzan often, and yet the grief now, more than three years after her death, is short in its duration in most cases. Invariably my focus shifts from how much I miss her to how much I love her and the joy and delight she brought into my life. That shift of focus seems to come more readily and more quickly as time passes.

While we do not forget a departed loved one—and I certainly would never choose to do that even if it were possible—I do believe that God, in His wisdom and mercy, knows that no person can sustain a high level of grief on an ongoing basis and remain effective in fulfilling God-given responsibilities to worship Him and to bless others. He moves quickly to bring to our minds the truth of His Word, the assurance of His presence, and the reminders of the joys that lie ahead for us and our loved ones.

My feelings of grief do not hang around as long as they once did, and my emotions seldom reach the intensity they once reached. In that, I see the grieving process as running its natural course. I have no desire either to prolong or to shorten the process that God is orchestrating in me. Slowly, and yet surely, He is replacing my sorrow with His joy and with a more ever-present awareness of the everlasting promises of Christ.

19

CHOOSING
THE BEST
MEMORIES

ONE AFTERNOON, Cindy, Julie, the Redhead, and I
had an opportunity to revisit a home we bought when we
first moved to Dallas. We had spent seventeen years there.
The house was being refurbished, and the Realtor invited
us to stop in and walk through it if we wanted to. As I
walked into the backyard to look at the swimming pool and
to marvel at how much the trees had grown in the eleven
years since we had lived there, I thought about how much I
had enjoyed swimming in that pool and chipping golf balls
with Tom in the yard.

I reflected as I walked through my first small home
office that I had written *See You at the Top* and *Confessions of
a Happy Christian* in that home. I relived some of the
moments I enjoyed in the much larger office that we created out of a portion of the original garage. The rest of the
garage had been converted into a playroom with a combi-
nation pool table and Ping-Pong table, and I remembered
the countless hours we had enjoyed in that room. Touring

the rest of the house, I vividly recalled my excitement at being able to buy that home, which we considered to be luxury beyond belief and bigger than anything we had ever dreamed of owning.

Then I went into the den area and stood in the exact spot where the Redhead stood the evening I gave her the news that Suzan had accepted Christ as her Savior. I relived the gratitude and joy I had felt in that moment.

In many ways, my memories of good times with Suzan are a lot like my revisiting of that old house. Every room and every area of the yard of that home were filled with good memories. So, too, are the years I had with Suzan.

A CHOICE OF WHAT TO REMEMBER

I have discovered in my grieving that life is a series of choices. I can lament the fact that I will never eat another of Suzan's pecan cookies, or I can choose to recall the good times when she baked them for me. I can grieve over the fact that I will never have another conversation on this earth with her, or I can be profoundly thankful for all the conversations we had. I can lament the fact that I do not hear her laughter, or I can rejoice at the number of times I did hear it.

In the same way, I can choose to grieve over the fact that Suzan was denied the opportunity of guiding Katherine through her teenage years, or I can rejoice over the fact that Suzan has laid in Katherine's life a strong foundation of faith, moral character, and sound values—a foundation on which her father continues to build.

I can choose to weep over the fact that Suzan will never be with us at our favorite vacation spot in Myrtle Beach, South Carolina, or I can look back with fondness and pleasure at the times we did have there together, especially the last time we were there.

Many things related to grief are choices. Will we choose to place our focus on missing the person or giving thanks for the gift of God that the person was to us?

ISOLATING THE TOP THREE MEMORIES

My wedding anniversary is usually a day when I feel very upbeat, optimistic, enthusiastic, and grateful for all that God has placed in my life. It is also a time for reflection.

In November, a little more than six months after Suzan's homegoing, the Redhead and I went to our home at Holly Lake to celebrate our forty-ninth wedding anniversary. We had a quiet, relaxing, and delightful time together. Each of us did a lot of reading, primarily on the subject of grief. The two books I had been reading about the grieving process had been helpful and encouraging, but they had reminded me of Suzan to the point that the memories brought tears. Many of those memories were rooted in the way Suzan felt and looked and acted in the days immediately before her death. I decided that weekend that I was going to refocus my memories to reflect on the happy times we shared, and I specifically decided that I was going to isolate and reflect upon the three times in which I felt Suzan had been the happiest.

The first of those happy times was when we lived in Stone Mountain, Georgia. Suzan became interested in horses, and I bought her a little Welsh pony. From my standpoint, the pony turned out to be a painful purchase. We learned several years later that the woman we trusted as a friend had taken advantage of our excitement and ignorance about the value of the horse, and we subsequently had grossly overpaid. Since we had sacrificed and struggled to pay for the little pony, the overpricing, combined with the feeling of betrayal, was difficult to deal with. We also learned later that the pony was not a good choice for a little girl. The pony was cantankerous and actually bit Suzan on the shoulder, which was particularly frightening to us because had his bite been better aimed, he might have maimed Suzan for life. All of my concerns and disappointments faded, however, in the delight and gratitude Suzan felt for the pony. The joy on her face and the expressions of love and exuberance she showed toward the animal were truly good memories. Suzan loved that mean little pony.

The second happy memory came from the days when we lived in Nashville, Tennessee. Again, that was not a particularly happy time from my perspective. I spent ten frustrating months working with a new insurance company that was unprepared to be launched. Nothing was in place and there was almost nothing to sell, so once again we were struggling financially. At the time we made the decision to move from Nashville, we heard about a family that had a Scottie puppy for sale. We stopped by "just to look" at the puppy and then impulsively bought it. The price was high, though reasonable compared to other purebred Scotties, but since we were struggling, it made no sense to buy the little dog. When I got that puppy home, the delight on Suzan's face was incredible—her joy was unbounded, her enthusiasm was spontaneous, her love, kisses, and displays of affection were unbridled that this truly became one of the moments of "Suzan happiness" that I have never forgotten.

The third memory involved her graduation from high school. I had promised Suzan a new car, but as seemed to be the pattern, we again were at a stage where we were struggling financially, although not nearly as much as we had in the past. The purchase of the car was a challenge for us. I believe what delighted Suzan so much was that she knew we were getting her the car despite the financial struggle. It also tickled her that the car she wanted was to be found only in Atlanta, and I was willing to go there and pick it up. I left Atlanta for the drive back to Columbia, South Carolina, at approximately one o'clock in the morning so Suzan would have her car at the crack of dawn on the day she graduated. I arrived home a little before five o'clock. And there she was, in the driveway, waiting for me! She had stayed up all night awaiting with much anticipation the arrival of her cherished gift. It was a Pontiac GTO, a "hot" car of the time. Her expressions of love, gratitude, appreciation, joy, and exuberance were sights and sounds I have never forgotten.

Reflecting on these happy moments, I couldn't help noting that they were initially difficult times for me. For Suzan, however, they were moments of pure bliss. In a way, my grief for Suzan has followed a similar pattern. The struggle is *mine*, not Suzan's. The darkest months and years of my life since her homegoing have been difficult for me, but for Suzan, who is living in the light of all eternity, this has been only a prelude of exceedingly great joy to an eternity that will be filled with ongoing unbounded joy.

In refocusing my mind on the moments of great happiness in Suzan's time, I found myself concentrating on the intensity of our joy in having Suzan as a daughter rather than on the shortness of our time with her. The truth is, no matter how long we had shared life with her on earth, the time would have been too short. The bright silver lining to our grief lies in the fact that we will have eternity with her, and that eternity will have no dark clouds in it.

RINGSIDE SEATS FOR
AN ENTIRE LIFETIME

From the moment Suzan entered our lives, just two and a half years after our wedding, she was in on everything we did. She was there to share our joys and triumphs, failures and successes, friends and acquaintances, business ups and downs, and honors and accomplishments. She participated in family discussions, business discussions, writing discussions, and virtually all other discussions that have been instrumental in molding us as a family.

In like manner, we were there in Suzan's life. We had ringside seats for all of her life. What a privilege it is to be able to see the whole lifetime of a person you deeply love!

The Redhead and I watched her go through many trials and tribulations in her sickness, but we had also known Suzan in times of abundant energy and health. We had watched Suzan grow and mature from a baby into a young woman. We had watched her grow in her marriage to Chad. We had observed the love and care she showered upon Katherine and Elizabeth. We had witnessed her enthusiasm for her faith rooted in Jesus Christ. We had watched her grow in her faith and become an example to others. I had come to respect her highly as a coauthor and colleague in our work.

My memory is drawn frequently to numerous moments in Suzan's life that I recall with happiness.

When Suzan was only about two or three years old, I was playing with her one night, and she suddenly closed her eyes. I spontaneously said to her, "Don't do that, Suzie. When you close your eyes, everything goes dark and I need to see!" She laughed and instantly closed her eyes again, and we played that game for a few minutes. We repeated that process several times over the following weeks.

Out of fear that someone might do the same ridiculous thing, I hesitate to mention something that is very dangerous and is now against the law. Suzie would sit on my left leg as I drove the car. In those days before cars were air-conditioned, we would usually have the windows rolled down. Suzie delighted in sticking her hand out the window, grabbing air, and putting it in my mouth. It was a game we played—one of the joys of having my little girl ride in the car with me.

Like most first-time fathers, I always extolled Suzan's virtues and told everyone about the cute and witty things she said and did. To me, she was *obviously* the most beautiful child in the history of mankind, easily the most personable, undoubtedly the brightest, and certainly the most fun of any child ever born.

When we were living in Florence, South Carolina, and I was putting on cookware demonstrations, the woman who helped me was Harriet North. Her daughter, Janice, was a few months older than Suzie. Much to my disbelief, Harriet seemed to think that Janice possessed all the qualities our Suzie possessed—and then some. Harriet and I were always involved in one-upmanship regarding our daughters, and we had a good time boasting about them.

I might have conveniently forgotten some of Harriet's victories, but I certainly claimed victory on two significant occasions. One morning about nine o'clock, the Redhead had gone to the grocery store to pick up a few items, and I was looking after Suzie. Suddenly a brainstorm hit, and that's always a dangerous time for me. I picked up the telephone, called Suzie, who was two and a half at the time, into the bedroom where the phone was located, sat her down on the bed next to the phone, and dialed Harriet's phone number. Then I stepped down the hallway a few feet, knowing I could hear the answering of the phone by Harriet on the other end. The minute she picked up the telephone I went stomping those last few feet and said to Suzie, "Suzie, how many times have I told you to leave the telephone alone? Have you called someone else?" With that, I took the phone from her hand and said, "Hello?" Harriet recognized my voice and said, "Zig, is that you?" I replied, "Hello? Who is this?" Harriet laughed and said, "It's Harriet! Did Suzie dial this number?" I laughingly said, "Well, I guess she must have. She's always calling somebody." For a long time I kept Harriet in the dark about that prank.

Another time when our families were together and little Janice's grandparents were also present, Mr. North began pointing out some of the brilliant things that Janice was doing. I listened patiently and smilingly said, "Yes, I know exactly how you feel because I well remember when Suzan was going through that stage herself." Janice, of course, was a few months older than Suzie, but I couldn't miss an opportunity to engage in a little one-upmanship, even if it wasn't entirely accurate.

Some of the things that I miss most about Suzan and that I recall with the greatest happiness are not the things that you might suspect. I miss . . .

- the beautiful interchanges we had as we discussed the best way to express something or when she gently persuaded me that there was a better, more loving, kinder, gentler way of expressing an idea. I had great respect for Suzan's intellect, which was substantial, but I had an even greater respect for her heart filled with love.

- her infectious laugh that seemed to fill an entire room or an entire day with joy. On one occasion, the Redhead turned on a recording that our children had made one time when they were all at Del Frisco's Steak House. A voice that came through loud and clear was Suzan's—her frequent and spontaneous laughter carried a natural and enormous enthusiasm, filled with life and delight and gratitude. Yes, I miss the sound of her laughter!

- seeing Suzan at work in the kitchen. Suzan loved eating good food and cooking for large groups of people. I think some of her happiest moments were spent in the kitchen, surrounded by family and friends.

As I thought over happy times with Suzan, I recalled one rare experience when I drove her from Texas to South Carolina to attend the university. We were driving in a sparsely populated area late at night when we had car trouble. I was particularly glad that I was driving because the car literally quit running in the middle of nowhere. Suzan was astonished that I did not seem upset or concerned. Instead I reminded her that we had passed a gas station a mile or so back. I expressed my hope that it would still be open when we got there, and sure enough, we walked back to it, got the help we needed, and were again on our way. She seemed to think that entire experience was an adventure.

If somebody, under any circumstance, said anything even mildly unkind about me, Suzan would furiously defend her dad. On one occasion when she felt somebody had "done me wrong," she wanted to go to that person's place of business and lead a protest march! I always thought it was funny, but needless to say, I was pleased that she felt that way about her daddy. And I was also pleased that she didn't actually carry out her plans for the protest!

I recall with happiness how much Suzan loved snow. The harder it snowed, the better she liked it. The first hint of snow or a drop in temperature or a weather forecast of the possibility of snow brought out the five-year-old child that still lived in Suzan's heart, even as an adult. Her excitement and enthusiasm about the possibility of the ground being covered with snow delighted me. She loved to build snowmen. She laughingly said on more occasions than I can count that she was going to do her "snow dance" to bring more snow.

I have vivid memories of one of the first snowfalls Suzan experienced. We had recently bought her a beautiful little green outfit with a nice button-down coat that had a high collar, a warm little hat that covered her head and ears, and leggings that zipped at the bottom and tucked under her feet. With her blonde hair sticking out from under that hat, she made a stunningly beautiful picture. I recall watching her play in the snow in Knoxville, Tennessee, loving every minute of it—the feel of the snow in her hands and on her face, the crunch of walking through the snow, the delight at catching snowflakes, the fun of scooping up handfuls of snow to throw.

One January day after Suzan died, I was watching the snow come down and was reminded of her. I called my family at the lake and told them that Suzan was doing her "snow dance." My daughter Julie responded quickly, "Oh, boy, we can have happy Suzie thoughts all day!"

A LEGACY OF JOY

Just about a year after Suzan died, I had occasion to play golf with Scott Mack, George Bjorkman, and my pastor, Dr. Jack Graham. It was a most enjoyable day. Scott had written a nice letter to me, detailing the impact of my work on his life. He was most kind and gracious in his comments, and I was encouraged and grateful that God has used me to help others.

At the end of the day, as we were preparing to depart the course, George and I had a few moments together. He said, "I have a message for you. My wife was on duty when Suzan was in Plano Hospital." George went on to tell me that his wife had been a nurse for eleven years and that she had never witnessed a family that displayed as much joy and laughter, or that loved one another and the Lord as openly as our family had. Her emphasis repeatedly was on the *joy* she witnessed in us. He said we had ministered to his wife in a wonderful way.

I could hardly respond to George. Tears were flowing freely from my eyes.

Reflecting on this discussion later, I came to several conclusions. One was that we were as joyful and laughed as much as we did because we did not realize just how sick our Suzan was. Even so, I believe Suzan knew in her heart that the end of her life was near. I also believe that her joy at seeing the Lord in the near future helped balance the sadness she felt at leaving her family behind.

I believe that Suzan wanted to leave a memory of joy in the mind of each loved one. Her spirit and laughter were totally contagious, and she had an ability to lift the spirits of others, including those of her family. In many ways, our laughter as a family was a reflection of Suzan's laughter.

What a wonderful thing it is to leave a legacy of joy. What an enviable thing it is to have others see the joy of loving and serving Christ in all that you do.

I also came to the conclusion that the day of golf I had just experienced would have given Suzan joy. Why? The occasion for the golf game was to benefit the Prestonwood Baptist Church Crisis Pregnancy Center. A game of golf with Pastor Graham and me had been offered in a silent auction and George and Scott had been the highest bidders. The Sunday prior to our golf game, three rosebuds had been placed on the platform directly in front of the pulpit in the church auditorium, each one representing a life that had escaped the abortionist because of the love expressed to young mothers through the Crisis Pregnancy Center. I know that Suzan would have been thrilled to know that what was happening that day had been for a significant cause. I know she would have been joyful that three babies born that week had been given the gift of life.

We who remain on this earth after the death of a loved one have a responsibility to exhibit joy and to do what our loved one would have counted as joy. To express joy is one of our highest callings in Christ. It certainly is one of the greatest memorial gifts we can give to a loved one who has died in Christ.

The freedom of choice is one of our most precious gifts, and I encourage you to choose to have joyful memories today of the loved ones you may have lost. Choose *joy* as their legacy to you. It is one of the most wonderful gifts you can give to yourself in their memory.

20

CAN A PERSON PREPARE IN ADVANCE FOR GRIEF?

Is THERE A way a person can prepare for grief, an experience virtually everyone will go through at some time in his life?

No, I don't believe you can deliberately prepare in advance for grief. And yet, there is a preparation. It lies in the way you attempt to live your life from the moment you make a commitment to Christ.

I am convinced that all grief, not just that of losing a child, can be more effectively dealt with if you in your own mind and heart truly know Christ as Lord. This knowledge gives you the assurance that you will spend eternity with Him, and with that assurance you've just removed a major cause for worry from your mind.

The psalmist proclaimed, "Happy are those who are strong in the Lord, who want above all else to follow your steps. When they walk through the Valley of Weeping it will become a place of springs where pools of blessing and refreshment collect after rains! They will grow constantly in strength and each of them is invited to meet with the Lord in Zion" (Ps. 84:5–7 TLB).

The psalmist added, "A single day spent in your Temple is better than a thousand anywhere else! I would rather be a doorman of the Temple of my God than live in palaces of wickedness. For Jehovah God is our Light and our Protector. He gives us grace and glory. No good thing will he withhold from those who walk along his paths" (Ps. 84:10–11 TLB).

Yes, our preparation for grief lies in the way we choose to live our lives in Christ. It also lies in our answers to some very basic questions:

- What kind of person am I, and what kind of person do I want to be?

- What do I believe?

- What kind of relationships do I have with my family members, friends, neighbors, and coworkers?

- What would be the impact on my life of the sudden loss of a person whom I have wronged?

The next step is one that I took and that, by now, is probably obvious: tell people who are dear to you about Christ, His love for them, and His sacrifice for them. Use verses from this very book and examples from this confession, and share your faith with that person. Then if a loved one goes home to meet the Lord unexpectedly, you will have made the best possible preparation for handling your grief.

WHAT WILL I EVENTUALLY WANT
TO FEEL AND KNOW?

On the day after Suzan's funeral, the question entered my mind, *Should I shift my thinking and focus on things other than the loss of my daughter and the keen sadness I feel at that loss?* At first, the idea that I might do this seemed almost unthinkable and, to a degree, disrespectful to Suzan and traitorous to my heart. Then I thought about the many positive aspects related to Suzan's death that were worthy of my focus.

What were these positive facets?

The first positive facet was that I had no fear about Suzan's entrance into eternal life. I had no fear that she might not be with the Lord, that she might be in pain, or that she might be anyplace other than heaven. What a positive and wonderful thing it is to know with complete assurance that Suzan is with the Lord and is whole, alive, and vibrant in the eternal life that lies before her.

The second positive facet was that I had no regrets about my relationship with Suzan. I had the full confidence that I loved her as much as any father could love a daughter and that Suzan knew that I loved her with all my heart. What a wonderful thing it is to have absolutely no "if only" or "I regret" thoughts.

The third positive facet was that I had no faith-shattering doubts about God's purpose, timing, or love. I felt highly confident that God was in complete control of every aspect of Suzan's life and homegoing. I will never fully know all God's purposes, but I was and am content in *not* knowing. I trust God that He did the most loving, perfect thing on Suzan's behalf in calling her home at the time He did. I can only imagine how emotionally troublesome it would be to be filled with doubts and questions about God's goodness and love in the face of a loved one's death.

The fourth positive facet was that I had no anger. I had no anger at any person I believed should have or could have done more to prolong Suzan's life. I had no anger at God for calling her home. God is sovereign and He is providential. Not only is He the King of this universe and of our personal lives, but He does all things for His purposes and according to His plan. God always operates out of love and is always motivated by a desire to do what is the very best for our eternal good. How can a person be angry at a loving God who truly works all things for good to those who are called according to His purposes?

My tears have been tears of sadness, not tears born of fear, doubt, frustration, or anger. And for that I am grateful. How wonderful it is to find something for which to be grateful in the midst of sorrow!

Truly, I cannot imagine how much harder it would have been if these positive aspects related to Suzan's death had not been present. Yes, these positive things were worthy of reflection and of thanksgiving to God. And even more important, they are positive aspects of life that are a preparation for future grief.

The question each of us can ask is this: How will I want to feel and what will I want to know with certainty after a loved one dies? The answer for me is fourfold:

1. I will want to know that my loved one is with Christ and that we will be together again one day.

2. I will want to know that I have done my very best to express my love, and that I have no regrets and no unforgiveness in my relationship with my loved one.

3. I will want to be confident in my faith that God has acted out of love in fulfilling His purposes and His plan in my loved one's life.

4. I will want to harbor no anger, frustration, or resentment in my heart.

To live in a way that wins others to Christ, that expresses Christ's love and my love to others—and to do my best to live in a state of forgiveness and strong faith—*is* excellent preparation for the grief that may come in my life. To live this way is not only the best way to face and to prepare for the inevitability of grief; it is the best way to *live*!

POSTLUDE

*C*ONFESSIONS OF A GRIEVING CHRISTIAN has centered almost entirely on the feelings my family and I have had about the loss of Suzan. However, as I have written this book and talked with countless numbers of people, I've come to realize there are innumerable kinds of grief that are as real, though perhaps not as intense, as the loss of a child. With this in mind, I'm doing some preparation and research for writing yet another book on grief of differing kinds.

If you have suffered deep mental anguish or sorrow over a loss and would be willing to share how you've dealt with that grief, it would be helpful to many people. Chances are good that virtually everyone who reads this book has grieved over a number of different things and I will include many of them, but I can't possibly include all of them. High on the list would be the loss of a parent, sibling, or mate. Close behind would fall the loss of a good friend, a mentor, a favorite aunt, uncle, cousin, grandparent, or grandchild.

The list is long: divorce; a home destroyed by fire, flood, or earthquake; a debilitating illness or accidental disability (loss of limb, sight, or hearing); the loss of a hope or dream when a child becomes addicted to drugs, alcohol, or gambling; an unmarried child involved in an unwanted pregnancy. Grief could come by way of a family member who was sent to prison or who injured or killed someone; maybe someone you loved became involved in organized crime. Perhaps a parent or close relative suffered a mental illness—Alzheimer's or dementia. Possibly someone you love became paraplegic following a serious accident. The loss of a job or even retirement can bring on grief, as can the loss of a beloved pet.

Grief is real and some forms of grief perhaps never end, but there are ways that help us to accept and live with them. If you've had any experiences with handling grief that you feel would be beneficial to others, you can make a significant contribution by sharing with our readers exactly how you dealt with that grief. Please send your story and suggestions to:

Ziglar Training Systems
3330 Earhart #204
Carrollton, TX 75006
FAX # 972-991-1853

APPENDIX

Suzan Ziglar Witmeyer
Funeral Service
May 16, 1995

Rick Brisco:
"Because He Lives"

John West:
Because He lives, we can live forever. I think that's the message and the good news that we all need to hear today, isn't it? We're here to celebrate the life of Suzan Witmeyer. Suzan was born on May 10, 1949, in Lancaster, South Carolina, and Jesus came and took her home to be with Him this past Saturday morning.

Suzan's life and her death are a testimony to the goodness and grace of God. You know, sometimes we just don't understand, do we? This past week at the hospital I watched a husband open the precious Word of God and read to his wife. Word after word, Scripture after Scripture, he just read God's Word to her. I watched a mom and a dad pray for their daughter. I watched them kiss her and embrace her and tell her over and over how much they loved her. I watched and listened to two sisters and a brother sing and pray. I'll tell you, Jesus was all over that hospital.

I watched this family during this difficult time love one another. You see, I believe God uses times like this for us to kind of hold on to those folks that we need to hold on to. And I listened as they talked about old times and good times. There was a whole lot of hugging, crying, and praying. But we also took time to laugh some. Jean said that Suzan loved parties and that she would really love all that was going on there in her hospital room.

I want to share a verse of Scripture with you. Jesus was about to go be with His Father. His disciples didn't totally understand what was happening, and Jesus shared these words with them and I want you to listen closely because I believe that these words are applicable to each one of us today. Jesus said, "Let not your heart be troubled; you believe in God, believe also in Me. In My Father's house are many mansions; if it were not so, I would have told you. I go to prepare a place for you. And if I go . . . I will come again . . . that where I am, there you may be also" (John 14:1–3 NKJV). And Thomas doubted. He didn't understand. And Jesus said, "I am the way, the truth, and the life: no man cometh unto the Father, but by me" (John 14:6 KJV).

Isn't it good news to know that Jesus gives us a supernatural peace? He says, "Let not your heart be troubled." But He gives us a place. He says, "In My Father's house are many mansions." And then He gives us a promise. He says, "If I go I'll come again that where I am, there you may be also." But then He gives us a pathway. He doesn't leave us without the way. He says, "I am the way, the truth, and the life: no man cometh unto the Father, but by me."

You know, one of the things that I saw in this family this past week, through it all, through everything that happened, there was a scarlet thread of love and joy. There was a supernatural peace because, you see, each member of this family has accepted Jesus Christ as their personal Lord and Savior, and they believe that there is a heaven.

Let's pray together:

Lord, we just thank You for life. And, Lord, we thank You that You made provision for us, that those who trust in You, that when we close our eyes here we open them up in heaven, and Lord, I thank You for that promise, that provision. Lord, I thank You for this family. I thank You for the encouragement they are to other people. I thank You for the love and the hope that they have in their lives because of Your love for them. And, Lord, I thank You for each person who's come here today. Lord, many have come from many, many miles away to encourage this family. Lord, I pray that this hour, they will hear a word from You. Lord, I thank You that You came to give us life, both abundant and eternal. In Jesus' name, amen.

Rick Brisco:
"Oh, What a Moment When We See Christ"

Jim Lewis:
Today we are experiencing one of those times in life where we have two very contrasting emotions. On the one hand, we are here—especially the family—going through a time of grief and loss. And it is very real. But on the other hand, we have come today and we are experiencing hope. And it is also very real.

This past two weeks, being with the family, I think that's the thing that I saw all the way through with Chad and the Ziglar family. A sense of grief but a sense of hope

all the way through it. And now, in God's providence and
sovereignty in calling Suzan home, we are reminded of
what the apostle Paul said in 1 Thessalonians 4:13 (paraphrase) concerning our facing the death of loved ones:
"We grieve, but not as others without hope." Our grieving
has hope. And today I know the family is here, grieving,
but with real hope. And that hope comes from faith in
God. Hebrews, chapter 11, verse 1 (paraphrase) says that
"faith is the evidence of things hoped for, and the conviction of things not seen. Faith brings the unseen reality of
God into the seen realities of this life." And that's what's
happening here today; that's what's happening with this
family.

As we think of their hope today, I want to share with you
what I see in them and what we can share together. Hope in
at least three specific areas. I see in this family an unwavering hope concerning the mystery of Suzan's homegoing.
And let's face it head-on: we prayed, we sought God to heal,
we called upon Him and He chose not to; He chose to take
her home. And my mind cannot fathom why, taken in the
prime of life, this vibrant woman, so loved and so needed by
her husband, Chad, by her daughters, Katherine and
Elizabeth, by her mom and dad, Zig and Jean, by her sisters,
Cindy and Julie, and by her brother, Tom, and by so many
that needed her, depended upon her, and yet God said,
"It's time to come home."

And yet I see in this family a hope in the midst of this
mystery. I think it would be safe to say that this hope resides
in the fact that they believe that God is absolutely in control
of all things. They believe that He is a good God, is that not
right? And as we think about that, we face the simple dec-
larations of Scripture as well as the complex that tell us that
God is in control. I think of one passage like Psalm 103:19

(NASB) that says, "The LORD has established His throne in the heavens; and His sovereignty rules over all." Now, either that means what it says or it doesn't—but I believe it does. And what this verse is talking about is that God is sovereign and God is providential.

As we think of sovereignty, it simply means that God has the right to rule, based upon the essence of His character. Almighty God, Creator of the universe, all-knowing, all-powerful, ever-present. He has the right to rule. He is sovereign.

But providence ushers out of that and providence simply implies to us not only does He have the right to rule, but He does rule and reign over everything. And we can be assured that He rules and reigns with a predetermined eternal purpose that began before the foundation of the world and has manifested itself in time and space and in human history. It is revealing itself in our lives, in the life of Suzan, and it shall go on into the eons of eternity until one day it shall culminate with this great consummation of the glory of God. That's when all of creation will claim the perfection of our God and every knee shall bow and every tongue shall confess that Jesus Christ is Lord, to the glory of God the Father. At the heart, in the center of that plan, as mysterious as it is, God has also decreed that part of that plan will be to call out of this cesspool world a company of redeemed who have placed their faith in the Lord Jesus Christ. They believe that He died, believe that He arose, believe that He lives—and they, this company of the redeemed, shall share that glory with Him forever and ever.

We rejoice in that hope and this family rejoices in that hope that God is sovereign, God is providential, and it means this—and listen carefully. It means that God is absolutely in charge with an unwavering eternal purpose, and although He has allowed man certain freedoms, His sovereignty acts as an umbrella over those freedoms. We know this, that there is nothing that has happened, nothing that is happening, nothing that shall happen that does not harmonize with the eternal plan of God for His glory and our great good. My friends, that brings great comfort to us.

When we think of nothing happening without it being in harmony with God's eternal plan, that includes last Saturday morning at 9:45 when, in His providence, He called Suzan to Himself. And I stand like you, I don't understand why. It is a mystery. And yet God has told us in His Word, Isaiah 55:8–9 (NASB), "My thoughts are not your thoughts, neither are your ways My ways. . . . As the heavens are higher than the earth, so are My ways higher than your ways, and My thoughts than your thoughts." And for me, trying to get it in my simple understanding, I think God is saying, "I am God and you are not." And we bow before that truth.

I don't know of anything that can bring us more comfort than believing that God is sovereign and God is providential, but also I don't know of anything that can frustrate us any more if we do not get the balanced picture. What makes it possible for us to take the harshness of a rule in mystery and bring peace and hope out of it? It is this: when we think of the most high God ruling and reigning, let's not see Him as a God who indiscriminately rules in an impersonal way, but we have a God who rules in all the perfection of His character and we believe both truths, the Most High who is also loving, who is also just, who is also wise . . . He is gracious; He is merciful; He is good; He is compassionate. As we bring these characteristics of the Most High together, we can rest in the mysteries of life and declare Him to be good.

For me, when I face mysteries like this one we are facing today, I find it helpful to see God in two ways. First, to see Him most high, sitting on the throne, but then to also see another scene and to see Him as the One lying as a babe in a manger in Bethlehem. He is the same God in each picture. To see Him, high and lifted up, sitting on His throne . . . and then to see Him as that gentle young man who walked the roads of Galilee and the dusty streets of Jerusalem and ministered to people, the One who healed the sick, touched the leper, who held the children, who spoke of hope and declared, "In this ministry I came not to be served but to serve and to give my life a ransom for many." The scene that helps me most in the mystery, and which I hope will be an encouragement to you today, is to see this One high and lifted up, Ruler, Sovereign of the universe, but also to see Him as the One hanging naked on a criminal's cross, crying, "My God! My God! Why hast Thou forsaken Me?"—to know that He was there to give us hope, to give us confidence, to give us life. Let's remember as we see Him in these capacities that He is not lying in a tomb, but He is seated at the right hand of God the Father, a place of absolute control of His universe. He was in control on Saturday morning and He is in control today.

Hope in the control and the character of God. I have found this—that there are many unanswered questions of life, and when we face them, it's as if we are walking up to a deep, dark chasm and looking down into it. We look as intently as we might, but we cannot see the bottom; we cannot answer the question of Suzan's homegoing. But I believe this with certainty—we have a choice to either shake our fist in defiance and accuse God of being unloving, unjust, and unconcerned, or of falling on our knees and worshiping God and saying, "God, we will let You be God."

All through this ordeal of Suzan's sickness, that was her hope and her stay. She was willing to let God be God.

First Peter 4:19 (NASB) says, "Let those also who suffer according to the will of God entrust their souls to a faithful Creator in doing what is right." This family believes God has done what is right in His providence, in His sovereignty. And do you know something? In the mysteries of life there is going to be a day when the end of God's glorious plan will justify all of the mysterious means that He has used in accomplishing His plan and purpose on this earth.

Why? Have you ever said, "You know, I'm going to ask God about that one when I get to heaven. I need to find out what was behind all of that"? You know what I suspect? When we get to heaven and we see Jesus in all of His glory, in all of His majesty, in all of His splendor, there will be but two words that we will say concerning the questions of life: "Of course." *Of course!* One glimpse of Him will be all that we shall need for the rest of eternity concerning the mysteries of life.

What a God! What a hope! This family has that hope this morning. But there is another hope they have. It's what the Scriptures call "the living hope." John was already referring to it in some measure. We find this recorded in the book of 1 Peter, "Blessed be the God and Father of our Lord Jesus Christ, who according to His great mercy has caused us to be born again to a living hope through the resurrection of Jesus Christ from the dead, to obtain an inheritance which is imperishable and undefiled and will not fade away, reserved in heaven for you, who are protected by the power of God through faith for a salvation ready to be revealed in the last time" (1:3–5 NASB). Jesus Himself said this in another way, talking of the living hope, speaking to a sister who was grieving over the death of her brother. He said to her, "I am the resurrection and the life; he who believes in Me shall live even if he dies, and everyone who lives and believes in Me shall never die. Do you believe this?" (John 11:25–26 NASB). These precious folks here believe this, and so do I. I know that many of us do. We have *living* hope.

Paul described this living hope in 2 Corinthians 5:8 (paraphrase) when he said, "When we are absent from the body we are home with the Lord." Let's make sure we understand that Suzan is not here. She is there, at home with the Lord. This is merely her body, the shell of the vibrant life that she had. But she is home with the Lord. They have this living hope as a family.

I love what Dwight L. Moody said many years ago, near the end of his life. Speaking to an audience, he said, "One of these days soon you are going to read that Dwight L. Moody is dead. Don't you believe it! I will be more alive at that moment than I have ever been!" The past few days you heard that Suzan Witmeyer is dead. Don't you believe it! She is more alive than she has ever been. She has gone on to be with the Lord, and she has experienced the victory that Jesus Christ won when He died, that He won when He arose, and that victory is hers and she is now in the unhindered glorious presence of God because she believed. This family has great hope. They know that she has gone on to glory.

The mortal life has been swallowed up by the immortal life; the temporary has given way to the eternal; the seen has given way to the unseen, and as Paul said in 2 Corinthians 4:17 (NASB), momentary, light affliction has produced for her "an eternal weight of glory far beyond all comparison." My friends, and precious family, as we prayed for Suzan to be healed, we were thinking in terms of physical healing, but she has been healed in ultimate healing; she has been healed with the glory of immortality. She shares at this moment the glory of God. As Paul said, to depart and to be with Christ is far better, and he also said in Philippians 1:21 (NASB), "For to me, to live is Christ, and to die is gain." That's what has happened here. That's the hope of this family.

Oftentimes when a person dies after a battle with a disease, we might say concerning Suzan, "Suzan Witmeyer lost her battle with pulmonary fibrosis." But that's not correct. She didn't lose. She gained. She won. She experienced the victory of the Lord Jesus Christ, and she now rests in the unhindered presence of God, experiencing things that we cannot imagine. I suspect that in light of where she is and what she is experiencing, if she could choose to come back, she would not, and if we love her and could see her as she is right now, we would not wish her back. She is in the place of ultimate destiny, the place that she was created to be, in the presence of Jesus Christ, her Savior, forever and ever, and that is the hope of these precious people here today.

This family has a hope of reunion with Suzan someday, maybe very soon. Chad, I suspect that heaven is more precious to you today than it was a few days ago. I suspect for the rest of the family that is also true. Because there is a precious one there waiting, and I'm sure that within the grief of these days you have already been experiencing a hunger for your own homegoing. She is there in the glory of God, and she is waiting for you. And we rejoice with you that you have this hope of reunion.

Hope in the midst of grief. Hope in the fact that God controls and God controls through the perfection of His character. The living hope that life here is temporary and simply gives way to the true life to come in Christ. But there is also a hope that I would like to encourage you with in the present, in the grieving. When the apostle Paul asked to be delivered from the thorn he experienced, God did not deliver him. Even so, Paul declared that the Lord spoke to him these words: "My grace is sufficient for you and My power will be perfected in your weakness" (2 Cor. 12:9 paraphrase).

Let me encourage all of you—Chad, Katherine, Elizabeth, Zig, Jean, Cindy, Julie, Tom—each of you. Grieve. Sorrow. Mourn your loss. It is real. Do not hold back the tears. They are part of the process. Weep. But in the weeping, believe that God is sufficient and His grace is sufficient. Turn to Him as the Shepherd who will provide all your needs. Look to Him as the Friend who will be closer than a brother. Grieve. Mourn. But allow God to bring hope and healing and encouragement and strength in the midst of your grieving.

For the rest of us, what shall we do for this family? Let us pray for them and let us grieve with them. Romans 12:15 (paraphrase) says, "We are to rejoice with those that rejoice and weep with those who weep." Sometimes I think we have this verse confused. We think that we in the body of Christ are to rejoice with those who rejoice and try to get those who are weeping to stop weeping and start rejoicing. That is not what the Scripture says. It says we are to weep with those who weep. Let us weep, then, with this family. This family does not need to hear our sermons or our glib quotations of Scripture in their weeping and mourning. Let's just be with them and weep with them and minister grace through our presence and pray for the ministry of God's Spirit. I encourage you today, grieve and mourn, but look to the sufficiency of God to minister to you.

If Suzan could speak today, what would she say to us? I

know one thing that she would say, "Do you know my Jesus? Do you know Jesus Christ in a personal way? Do you have the living hope?" She would say to us, as Jesus said to Martha that day, "I am the resurrection and the life; he who believes in Me shall live, even if he dies, and everyone who lives and believes in Me shall never die. Do you believe this?" And I ask you, do *you* believe this? I don't know all the people in this room, but certainly in an audience this size there would be one and maybe more who do not personally know Jesus Christ as your Savior and your Lord. I want to say this, there would be no higher tribute that you could pay to Suzan Witmeyer than to come to a saving relationship with Jesus Christ as a result of Suzan's homegoing. There would be no greater joy that this family could experience than to experience knowing that someone in this room had accepted Jesus Christ. Indeed, that is what this family is praying. I won't be surprised if their prayer produces a rich reality for them. *Do you know Jesus?*

I'm not talking about the facts of Jesus' life. I'm not talking about certain stories about Jesus. I'm talking about having a personal, living relationship with Him, one that brings forgiveness of sins and eternal hope. Do you know this One called Jesus Christ, the Lord? My friend, I don't know of a better time to examine the issues of eternity than right now when we're facing the reality of death. Death is real. So is eternity. Do you know Jesus Christ? That is the fundamental question and issue that must be answered. The decision of what we will do with Jesus determines not only the quality of our life here on earth, but it determines where and how we shall spend all eternity. We're not talking about things that are a fairy tale. We're talking about the greatest reality of life—what will we do with Jesus Christ? Do you know Him?

The Scriptures make it very plain. Romans 3:23 (KJV) says, "For all have sinned, and come short of the glory of God." That puts us in a very awkward position, we being sinners by nature and God being holy and righteous by His nature. The Scriptures say that because of that there is a great gulf between man and God, a great separation. There can be no intimacy with God in this life or in the life to come unless that gulf is spanned. Furthermore, not only are we separated in our natural condition, but we are under the judgment of God. The Word says, "The soul that sinneth, it shall die" (Ezek. 18:20 KJV). And in the Word, Romans 6:23 (KJV) says, "The wages of sin is death."

If we stopped right there in our reading of the Scriptures, we would be left with a pretty dismal, hopeless message, wouldn't we? But we don't stop there. In our sinful condition there is nothing any of us can do to gain God's favor. There is nothing we can do to bridge the gap to have a relationship with God. The gap goes all the way back to the beginning. After Adam and Eve fell, God made a promise that He would send a Redeemer, and the people of God waited and waited and waited. And some two thousand years ago that Redeemer came, and as unthinkable as it is, He was the eternal Son of God who stepped out of heaven to be born as a man, to live among us, and then to die on a criminal's cross in order that He might pay the debt and take the weight of your sin and mine on Himself, and die under the judgment of a holy, righteous Father. Jesus paid the debt for our sin. He finished the bridge from God to man. He did what we could not do. He settled our relationship before the justice of God.

Jesus died under the weight of sin and was buried, and three days later He arose triumphant from the grave—triumphant over sin, triumphant over hell. He lives today and offers forgiveness and restoration and right standing with God to those who will simply, by faith, put their trust in Him as Savior, and who put their hope in Him to put them in right relationship with God. I am so thankful that before Jesus died on the cross, He cried, "It is finished!" He was not saying that His life was finished. He was saying, "This debt has been paid!" When Jesus arose from the grave, it was as if God the Father confirmed, "This payment is accepted for the debt," and that's why the Scriptures say that Jesus Christ, when He arose from the grave, put an end to the agony of death. That's why there's a living hope. That's why there's relationship in this life and hope of the life to come for those who will put their faith and trust in Him.

It's not our works; it's not our doing. That's the beautiful part. The Scriptures say, "For by grace you have been saved through faith; and that not of yourselves, it is the gift of God; not as a result of works, that no one should boast" (Eph. 2:8–9 NASB). John 1:12 says that as many as receive Him, to them He gave the power to become, and the right to become, the sons of God. Let me ask you again, "Do you know Him? Wouldn't you like to know Him?"

Friend, if you are here today and you have never believed in the Lord Jesus Christ, I don't know of a better time than right now. You can turn to Him in the quietness of your heart, through a simple act of faith—yes, in the quietness of your own heart, you can say to Him in faith, "Yes, Lord, I believe. I recognize that I am a sinner. I believe that Jesus died, and by faith I trust Him to forgive my sins." You can do that even now. If Suzan were here, she would plead with you. As a representative of the Lord today, I implore you with all the earnestness that I possess, do not leave this room today without settling the issue of Jesus

Christ, now and for eternity, because the Scripture says those who reject Him not only are separated in this life, but for all the eons of eternity in the judgment flames—yes, of a place called hell. The bliss of heaven, the agony of hell. Joy and purpose in this life, or no hope in this life. Those are the alternatives. Will you believe? Will you trust in Him? The choice is yours.

For those of us who know Him, let us rejoice with this family in their hope. Let us pray with them. For those who do not know Christ, take this moment right now to turn to Him. Let us bow our hearts together in a moment of silence and each of us respond to God as the Lord may have prodded you, and then I'll close in prayer.

ABOUT THE AUTHOR

Zig Ziglar is chairman of the Zig Ziglar Corporation, which is committed to helping people more fully utilize their physical, mental, and spiritual resources. Ziglar is one of the most sought-after motivational speakers in the country. He travels around the world delivering his message of hope, humor, and enthusiasm to audiences of all kinds and sizes. He is the best-selling author of many books, including *Confessions of a Happy Christian, Something to Smile About, Over the Top,* and *See You at the Top,* which has sold more than 1.5 million copies worldwide. Zig and his wife, Jean, make their home in Dallas, Texas.

Look for These Other Books by Best-selling Author Zig Ziglar

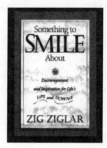

Something to Smile About

This delightful book is designed to be read a page each morning or evening by those who seek a word of encouragement, an uplifting thought, or positive reinforcement. It is a powerful collection of inspiring stories that may change the way you live out your faith.

0-8407-9183-6 • Hardcover • 224 pages

Over the Top—Revised and Updated

This sequel to the best-seller *See You at the Top* has been revised and updated with pages full of on-target advice for maximum success and happiness. Ziglar identifies and shows precisely how to achieve what everyone desires most in life—to be happy, healthy, reasonably prosperous, and secure, and to have friends, peace of mind, good family relationships, and hope.

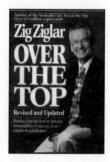

0-7852-7119-8 • Hardcover • 336 pages